The 10 Women You'll Be Before You're 35

alison james

Polka Dot Press
Avon, Massachusetts

Published by
Polka Dot Press, an imprint of
Adams Media, an F+W Publications Company
57 Littlefield Street, Avon, MA 02322. U.S.A.
www.adamsmedia.com

ISBN: 1-59337-277-9

Printed in the United States of America.

J I H G F E D C B A

Library of Congress Cataloging-in-Publication Data
James, Alison.
The 10 women you'll be before you're 35 / Alison James.
p.   cm.
ISBN 1-59337-277-9
1. Women—Psychology. 2. Socialization. 3. Life cycle, Human. 4. Developmental
psychology. I. Title: Ten women you'll be before you're thirty-five. II. Title.
HQ1206.J36 2004
305.4—dc22
2004019227

This publication is designed to provide accurate and authoritative information with regard to
the subject matter covered. It is sold with the understanding that the publisher is not engaged
in rendering legal, accounting, or other professional advice. If legal advice or other expert
assistance is required, the services of a competent professional person should be sought.
　　　　—From a *Declaration of Principles* jointly adopted by a Committee of the
American Bar Association and a Committee of Publishers and Associations

Many of the designations used by manufacturers and sellers to distinguish their products
are claimed as trademarks. Where those designations appear in this book and Adams
Media was aware of a trademark claim, the designations have been printed in initial
capital letters.

This book is available at quantity discounts for bulk purchases.
For information, please call 1-800-872-5627.

To Mom & Dad,

for helping me through every stage

acknowledgments

I would like to thank Danielle Chiotti, my editor, for her invaluable feedback and support; Gary Krebs, Beth Gissinger, Gene Molter, Karen Cooper and everyone at Adams Media for their time, energy, and dedication to putting together fantastic books; my sincerest appreciation to everyone who has contributed to this book, especially Vanessa and Tony Shuba; Tina, Jesse, and Patrick Reno; Colette Curran and Liz Leo; special thanks to Art Vomvas and David Zagin for their contributions to my "working girl" perspective. Last but not least, I would like to thank Thomas Howe for his patience, enthusiasm, humor, and support every step along the way.

Don't laugh at a youth for [her] affectations; [s]he is only trying on one face after another to find a face of [her] own.

Logan Pearsall Smith

contents

introduction

Have you ever admired a woman who seems perfect from afar? She's wearing a chic outfit and walks with all the confidence in the world. She carries herself like she's got it together. You imagine she's a magnet for good fortune, that things for her are always easy. But are they?

Even a woman who appears together on the outside will admit that her life has not always been perfect. She has had moments when she was completely unsure of herself. She has looked in the mirror and seen a blob, a wreck—a person she didn't even recognize. She has re-examined her place in the world time and again, revisited old photos and diary entries and thought "Oh my gosh! Did I look like that? Why did I waste so much time with him? What was I doing with my hair?" She is like every one of us, traveling the road from teen to queen, from prom to mom, from girl to "I'm turning 30 and I really think I'm going to hurl." It's an exciting, challenging journey of self-discovery.

Being a confident, cool woman with some semblance of sanity in today's world is an extremely difficult thing to do. It's easier to climb Everest in Manolo Blahniks than it is to balance all the pressures on your shoulders and walk the tightrope to the saner side of life. From the moment we leave college until we're grownups (age 25? 35? 92?), life is like a whirlwind sending a new challenge our way each day. We're bombarded with ambiguous men, friends that up and move to a new city or get married and fall off the face of the earth, a bank account that teeters on the edge of net positive, and a thousand diet plans to boot. On top of that, we are part of a generation that is both blessed and burdened by liberation and the mixed messages that came with it. "Make money!" "Build your career!" "Get married!" "Be sweet and feminine!" "Be spunky and energetic!" It's no wonder we feel like we've been a hundred different people by the time we're 35.

The 10 Women You'll Be Before You're 35 is a guide to identifying, understanding, and mastering each of the crazy, fun, and challenging phases in your life and taking from them the important lessons that will make you a more confident, happy person today. Whether you feel like a social maniac this year and just can't get enough nightlife or you're completely broke and sleeping in a bunk bed with your old college roommate, this guide will help you see the funnier and educational side of the phase you're in and the ones you can't believe you endured. So if you're asking, "Is it normal to go through this?" "Is this horrific time ever going to end?" or "Was I even conscious during my neon pink lipstick phase?" read on. You'll see that the answer to all of these questions is "yes!"

With a sense of humor and a little attitude, you can learn the lessons each phase offers and integrate this knowledge into your life. You'll realize that nothing you've done or will do along the way is a waste of time. Each experience is something you face for a reason, and it helps make you who you are today. So recall each of the phases in your life with a smile—even those that seem vile—and before long you will be the true, fabulous you with absolutely no regrets!

thenewgraduate
so naive you can't believe!

the new graduate at a glance

nickname
Kid, Dear, Honey, Sweetie

look
Eager, fresh-faced, and way too young to be working.

fashion
Cheap black pants, ponytail, white shirt, and denim jacket.
Baseball cap on weekends.

phrase
"When I was in school, we would . . ."

love interest
College boyfriend, who graduated a year earlier. He has lived
in the real world for a while, has a paycheck, and gets passes to
exclusive bars.

favorite songs
Senior year mix CD.

events/activities
Dinners she can't afford, college alumni get-togethers, and trips
to visit old friends.

friends
Anyone from school who moved to the same city she did;
random people she meets because she needs all the new
friends she can get.

life goal
To make it through this job for a year and then, ideally, go back
to school.

When her college days come to a screeching halt, the New Graduate is certain that adult life will be grand. She's convinced that guys will be mature, employers will be thrilled to have her onboard, and friendships will grow into higher levels of sisterhood. With the day-to-day frivolity of schoolgirl life left far behind, a world of opportunity is before her. But in her new postcollegiate life, things aren't quite as movie-set perfect as she imagined.

Even with paychecks and jobs, the guys are still holding beer pong tournaments. Her new boss can't remember her name and she feels disconnected from her old friends as they assimilate into their new jobs and lives. Instead of being a calm, collected adult she feels more like a kid on the first day of school again, but this time she's on her own.

The New Graduate phase is a challenging one full of surprises and "I never thought life would be this difficult" moments. If you're in this phase now, you know the mixed emotions that accompany it. If you've been through this phase in the past, you're probably thinking "Whew . . . I'm glad I made it through . . . but it would be nice to do it again knowing what I know now." While you can't go back and do it again, you can laugh at all the crazy feelings you had and enjoy the New Graduate phase from a more mature, enlightened perspective. This phase is the time in every girl's life when endless possibilities lie before her and she has the enthusiasm to pursue them. It's a phase that's as fabulous as it is frightening. It is a time to remember and celebrate.

Life in the Real World

Here's what it's like for the New Graduate: One moment she is sleeping soundly, dreaming of the exciting days ahead as a twenty-something with a paycheck. Then someone comes into her room, whips open the curtains, and wakes her up. She sees her surroundings for the first time under the bright lights of the real world and feels bewildered, exposed, and unpolished. She wonders, "Where the heck am I and how can I be so excited about the future one minute and so freaked out the next?" She feels like she went to sleep a college kid but woke up in an unfamiliar land.

> The future has a way of arriving unannounced.
>
> George F. Will

Like all New Graduates, she feels enthusiastic but overwhelmed, excited but terrified, grown up yet more naive than she was in grade school. This exciting but challenging time is typical of life as a new member of the adult world. When you're in it, you can expect to feel a number of conflicting feelings that make you a little nutty sometimes.

Enthusiastic but Overwhelmed

No more exams. No more senior-year beer fat. As the New Graduate embarks on the road to adulthood, she is sure she's going to look great, do her own taxes, figure out what a W2 is, and fall in love with the perfect guy. In short, she's ready to tackle the world as an adult and get on with her life.

But the real world is more difficult than she imagined it would be. She's tired of waking up at six in the morning and she's only been doing it for three months. Her old college boyfriend is being lame, going out with his new work buddies all the time and acting like he's back in high school. Her closest friends are spread across the globe, so she has to make new ones. And she's not even sure that the courses she took in college are going to help her get anywhere after all. They seem so impractical now. It's about this time that she starts to wonder if she should just go back to school and relax in the safety of that environment. But deep down, she knows it wouldn't be the same.

Job Insecurity

She's come out of school thinking she knows what kind of job she wants. And she thinks she knows how to get it. After all, she's smart, educated, and armed with advice from older siblings and friends. She's studied for four years, and she has all of the book experience she needs. Her professors have told her things like "You're a very smart young woman," and "With your talent, you will go far." And she wants to believe this. She knows she might not get the perfect job right away, but she knows what she wants to do and nothing is going to change that. Right?

The guy who cheated off me in chemistry makes a million dollars a year as a basketball player and I can't find a job.

Anonymous

Postgraduate Urban Success Legends — Myth or Reality?

- The girl who took a job at her father's firm and is already making a six-figure salary.
- The guy who won the scholarship to study biology in Japan and has since cured the common cold.
- The girl who got married to a rich foreign prince the summer after graduation.
- The guy who moved to a Third-World nation to teach English.
- The girl who posed for *Playboy* and made a million dollars off the publicity.
- The girl who moved to Hollywood and is already making guest appearances on a sitcom.
- The guy who started his own pizza delivery business and sold it to Domino's for millions of dollars.

On the other hand, she keeps meeting people who ask her the same types of questions: "Where did you go to school?" "What are you doing now?" "Do you like it?" These questions make her start to doubt her choices. This is a tough dilemma for a New Graduate. The truth is, even though she was lucky enough to find a job in her field, it's really not quite as scintillating as she thought it would be. She feels like she doesn't fit in. But it's what she worked four years to achieve! She just can't walk away now! Can she? To make matters worse, she keeps hearing stories about people who already have their lives figured out. They're always a friend of a friend, or those people whose success profiles are in the alumni newsletters her mom keeps forwarding to her. Are these stories real, or are they merely postgraduate urban success legends? Urban legend or not, they make the New Graduate feel dull in comparison.

Kid on the Inside

During the New Graduate phase, you're a full-fledged adult on the outside. You've moved into your very own place and have your own bills to pay. You're adjusting to working an eight-hour business day, and you're even getting up before noon on the weekends. You have a real job with a real title (even if it's the lowest on the office totem pole). The nostalgia of your past life is slowly fading, and when you visit campus, you feel like you're on the outside looking in.

On the flip side, you still feel like a kid. Nothing seems permanent yet. You feel small and lost in your new life. Your boss spends his weekends fixing up his house and you spend yours going out with friends to bars. Every T-shirt you own has a college logo on it. Your proud, hopeful parents gave you an engraved business card holder for graduation but you don't have any business cards yet. You're still living on ramen noodles and mac and cheese. You're in the adult world but not part of it. You're in your own strange postgraduate limbo land.

If a hacksaw ever flew through the lecture hall, it would chop off all the raised hands. So for safety reasons, I kept mine down.

— Anonymous

College to Real-World Lingo Translator

You hardly recognize your best friend when she dons a power suit and struts to the office. The "We miss you!" cards from mom and dad have been pushed aside by a lengthy new employee information packet. Now, to make matters worse, the adults around you are using the words you took for granted in new ways. The most familiar part of your life, your own language, is in disarray.

Have you noticed that people speak differently in the real world than they do in college? About a month after you have your diploma in hand you start to realize that the lingo just isn't the same. If you're having problems making the transition because you can't figure out what the heck those real-world people are talking about, use this translator to learn the new meaning of your favorite old terms.

KEG STAND

College Definition: The act of holding a frat boy upside down so he can drink nasty beer straight out of the barrel.

Real-World Definition: A beautiful varnished wooden beer holder the rich yuppie forty-something has in his basement.

LIKE

College Definition: A word used frequently in college conversation that adds no meaning to a sentence but somehow enhances communication. Example: He is like so hot and like not gay either.

Real-World Definition: A word that pops out of the New Graduate's mouth in meetings, making her feel like a total idiot. Example: This report is like so wrong. A word she learns to use in the proper way in the real world. Example: I don't like getting up every day at 7 A.M. I don't like working all summer. I don't like my boss's breath, which makes the ends of my hair fry when he leans over my shoulder and asks me what I'm working on.

CLASS

College Definition: A gathering of several students and a professor to discuss an important subject. Example: You are taking "The Philosophy of Nietzsche" too? I love that class. It is so practical and applicable to everyday life.

Real-World Definition: A quality most of the men the New Graduate meets do not have. Example: The guy had no clue, no manners, and absolutely no class.

QUAD

College Definition: The grassy area between dormitories or classroom buildings often covered with bikini-clad girls, guys playing Ultimate Frisbee, and football players lying on couches they dragged outside during warm weather.

Real-World Definition: The muscle group in the mid-lower thigh that turns to cellulite and looks awful in a short skirt if not exercised properly at the gym; that area of the leg prone to varicose veins.

COMMON

College Definition: A place shared by all roommates. Example: There's a party in the common room Saturday night. Who is that weirdo sleeping on the couch in the common room?

Real-World Definition: A word used often by women when describing how a date went. Example: The guy was a loser. We had nothing in common. He was a common thug with no common sense. Is it common to want to ditch someone five minutes into dinner?

EXAM

College Definition: One of several tests that occur twice a year, at the end of each semester. Students prepare for them rigorously with study, coffee, and late nights at the library.

Real-World Definition: A word that conjures thoughts of a doctor's office, old magazines, and a long painful sit in a waiting room. Example: Did you go for your dental exam this year?

READING

College Definition: The homework given by professors that usually involves so many pages you can't get through it all in a lifetime. Example: Did you do the reading? This week it was de Tocqueville's scintillating Democracy in America.

Real-World Definition: Voluntary entertainment that is neither long nor painful. Example: I'm reading the best trashy romance novel. I went on a date with a guy who doesn't have basic life skills, like using utensils and reading.

RENT

College Definition: An odd slang expression students use to refer to their parents. Example: My 'rents are coming to visit this weekend. Gotta clean the common room cause the 'rents will be here.

Real-World Definition: The dreaded monthly fee the New Graduate must pay to her building owner in exchange for a closet-sized space to sleep in. Example: My rent is almost equal to my monthly take-home pay.

MEAL PLAN

College Definition: A prepaid allowance that students use to buy food from college cafeterias for meals.

Real-World Definition: A plan for dinner that usually involves pizza, macaroni and cheese, and other easy-to-prepare items.

TAXES

College Definition: The extra percentage a store charges on top of a purchase when a girl buys a cute dress.

Real-World Definition: The heinous, long, and scary record of her income that she has to submit to the IRS on April 15 of every year.

The Adult Voice

The New Graduate struggles with her conflicting emotions for a while, feeling strong and grown up one minute and weak and childlike the next. She wonders if she's ever going to fit into the real world and get this whole adult thing down pat. But one day, she wakes up before her alarm goes off, slips on her new

● **understanding mom and dad** The New Graduate learns that two people, depending on their age, can see the world in different ways. As she's faced with her own adult situations, she begins to see her parents as peers with their own problems and issues. She realizes that her mom and dad want the best for her but they don't always have all the answers. She has to learn to rely on herself.

suit, and steps out of the house, briefcase in hand and a spring in her step. She doesn't feel like the awkward kid anymore. Suddenly, this adult thing makes a little more sense.

She understands why her boss is obsessed with figuring out which life insurance plan to buy and what a 401(k) is. A younger crew of new graduates look up to her because she knows how to use the fax machine and where to get the FedEx supplies. Somewhere along the way, she became part of the real world, a confident, mature working goddess with her whole life ahead of her.

If we don't change, we don't grow. If we don't grow, we aren't really living.

Gail Sheehy

The Voices in Your Head

As you assimilate into the adult world, you start to push your more impulsive, enthusiastic nature aside. Your conscience starts nagging you to deal with life the responsible, mature way. Even when your kidlike energy eggs you on to make your dreams a reality, this rational, adult voice can pop up and quell your spirit at the most inopportune moments. Nevertheless, you have to believe that if you strive for it, you're destined for greatness—whether your dream is owning your own company, marrying a prince, or debuting on the big screen. And believing is more than half the battle. So while the day-to-day struggles of adulthood make it increasingly harder for you to maintain your energy and spirit, you still can. As the kid voice and adult voice in your head duke it out, try not to let your adult voice win completely and stomp out your youthful enthusiasm.

Kid Voice: "It will be so easy for me to get the best job."
Adult Voice: "Your education alone is not enough to land you a great job. You've got to pay your dues."

Kid Voice: "I'm gonna be so freakin' rich."
Adult Voice: "You're lucky they offered you the position. So what if your wages will be just below that of migrant farm workers? Enjoy."

Kid Voice: "I'll be a famous superstar as soon as someone discovers me."
Adult Voice: "Get a real job with benefits and stop dreaming. That guy in the sunglasses and linen suit is a pimp, not an agent."

Kid Voice: "I'm so young. I have the world in front of me!"
Adult Voice: "Don't wear your hair in a ponytail at work. Try a bun instead, and wire-rimmed glasses. A mature fashion statement will get you the respect you deserve."

Kid Voice: "I will meet my husband at 25 and be married by the time I'm 27. Everyone is on this schedule, right? That's just the way life works."
Adult Voice: "Your 33-year-old former supermodel co-worker is still single."

Kid Voice: "My best college buddy and I are going to live next door to each other forever and ever."
Adult Voice: "The real world doesn't come with a face book, sororities, or dining halls. You have to make an effort to meet new people."

● am i back at square one? When you arrive in the real world for the first time and people treat you like you're a kid, you might feel as though you are back at square one. But remember that you know a lot more than you think you do and those skills will come in handy when you least expect it.

Dream Slayers

Okay, so it sounds like the name of the latest video game or a Keanu Reeves movie, but it's actually a term used to describe those forces at work in the New Graduate's life that stifle her enthusiasm, optimism, and "reach for the stars" attitude. These forces can come from the outside, in the form of pessimistic co-workers, rainy weather, or an evil boss. Or they can be internal forces, led by her fears and insecurities.

The dream slayers can stifle your creativity, make you second-guess your path in life, and eat your positive energy like a famished fat man. By recognizing these forces at work in your daily life, you can resist them and turn them around into something positive. After all, "adult" doesn't have to mean "negative."

The Dreadful Work Routine

It interferes with spa day. It throws a damper on your plans to join the "ladies who lunch." It's a very big pain in the butt. It's your job. After the excitement of having a "real" job wears off, you find that the repetition makes you weary. You wake up, go to work, sit down at your desk, turn on your computer, have

A certain naiveté, unburdened by conventional wisdom, can sometimes be a positive asset.

Harish-Chandra

Shake-Up Moves

If you have fallen into a dull "real-world" routine, try a couple of the following "shake-up" moves:

Call in sick. Just because you don't have Fridays off any more doesn't mean you can't take one on occasion and sleep till noon in some good 'ol footsie-wootsie slippers.

Take a trip. Get out of town for the weekend. Find an equally work-weary friend and hit the road in search of a sandy beach, pine-coned park, or faraway cocktail lounge.

Try new things. Invite an office buddy to be your partner at the wine tasting event you've always wanted to attend. Get him tipsy enough to hand over some good gossip about your boss.

Be proactive. Think of what your dream job would be and write a letter to someone really accomplished in that field just to see if she responds. If she doesn't, follow her around, or at least read about her.

Meet new people. Looking to meet new people? Try the increasingly popular online dating services or have your friends set you up.

Visit the fam. Mom and Dad might not seem so bad now that you're in dire need of a homecooked meal.

Refresh your wardrobe. Every two months move everything from the back to the front. Throw a castaway party. Each friend brings those items she wants to get rid of in exchange for other newly orphaned clothes.

Get adventurous. Skydive naked, or try a less exhilarating but more legal form of outdoor entertainment like biking along a river or jogging at the park.

---

a cup of coffee, and begin your day. At approximately 5 P.M., you shut off your computer, struggle to get home during rush hour, go to the gym, watch TV, eat dinner, and go to bed. Day in and day out, you step in time to the cadenced drum, playing the same role over and over again like a corporate zombie.

This ho-hum daily routine is dream slayer number one and it is glaringly bizarre to you as the New Graduate. After all, you just came out of a world where people see daylight regularly. So at this stage of the game, you're probably thinking: "Who invented this crappy work thing, and why don't I get my summers off?"

But then you get comfortable. The momentum of doing what you did yesterday, the day before, the week before, and the month before is addicting. If you stick to your routine, you don't have to take any risks, there are no uncertainties, and you don't have to put forth much effort to live your life. So you roll with it for a while. Until one day you realize that you can't remember going from home to work that morning because you've traveled the same route so many times before.

Monotony doesn't have to be your destiny. Just because your life has become more routine than it used to be doesn't

All I Ever Needed to Know About Working I Learned in High School

We don't endure high school drama for no reason. As painful as high school may have been at the time, the dances, athletic practices, lunchroom antics, and cliques teach us valuable lessons that apply to the professional world.

- Stroke a guy's ego once or twice and he'll eat out of your palm.
- Popularity definitely counts for something when you're trying to get to the top.
- If you really want to get a job done, ask the smart kid for help.
- Dress to kill or be labeled a geek.
- Don't date someone that you have to see every day.
- Never throw food in someone's face to achieve results.
- Being friends with the coach trumps a kick-ass performance during tryouts.
- When the buzzer rings, go home and don't look back.

• times change What you want today will not be the same as what you want in five years or ten years. After all, how many old ladies do you know who are just dying to buy the latest Brazilian bikini?

mean that you can't have fun or take chances. It's important to remember to break your routine every once in a while—step outside your comfort zone and take a walk on the wild side. Be spontaneous. Shake things up, baby!

No matter what, don't let your New Graduate optimism and energy fall by the wayside. Once it gets away from you, it is hard to get it back. Shake something up other than your morning coffee creamer, and keep your life exciting. Re-examine the situations you're in regularly and ask "Is this something I really want or am I merely comfortable and afraid to make a move?"

A good solution applied with vigor now is better than a perfect solution applied ten minutes later.

General George S. Patton Jr.

Notorious Naysayers

Notorious Naysayers can drive any New Graduate nuts with their advice. They predict that your youthful pursuits will run aground and that you'll eventually become resigned to some boring, professional path devoid of flavor and fulfillment. Notorious Naysayers often include your parents, who long for you to be responsible; chatterbox coworkers who feel the need to share their questionable wisdom; and older friends who mean well but don't always have all the right answers for you. While these Naysayers want to be helpful, they have a knack for saying the wrong thing.

Their gloomy words can get into your head, making you doubt yourself and your goals. When you encounter Naysayers, you'll have to work extra hard to ward them off with enthusiasm and sass.

The Notorious Naysayers can slay your dreams with their "Those things can't happen to people like you" attitude. The best thing you can do is trust your own instincts—someday things will work out for the best. In the meantime, you can nix the Notorious Naysayers by giving them a little verbal slap right back. Better yet, thank them for their kind advice and then push it out of your head so you have room for happier thoughts of success.

The Pragmatic Parent

Mom and Dad want you to use your education wisely, which means one thing: securing a practical job with benefits. So they tell you "Become an accountant, not an artist. You'll never make any money as an artist." If you're feeling the pressure from your parents, you can use one of these tactics to reassure them.

* Divert their attention with "Hey, did you see that cousin Harry is in prison? His parents must be really embarrassed."
* Stroke their egos with "I want to try something really different for a while. I know I can't achieve your level of success without striking out on my own and trying new things first."
* Offer kind reassurance with "I love you very much and I appreciate your input but I need to make my own decisions." Then offer examples of famous people who have gone their own way and succeeded.

● tip   People love to call the New Graduate by cute little nicknames. If someone calls you "dear" or "kid," respond by calling her "Doe" or "Little Goat" (or "Billy Goat" if she has a hairy chin).

To those of you who received honors, awards, and distinctions, I say, well done. And to the C students—I say, you, too, can be president of the United States.

George W. Bush

The Chatty Gloom-and-Doom Coworker

As you get to know your coworkers, they'll probably delight in strolling by your cubicle to make small talk. Beware of the Chatty Coworker who constantly complains about his job and wants you to join the complaint club by saying things like, "Oh, you're one of us now. You'll never get out of this place." He'll ask you about your life and your goals and offer up his opinions and insights, saying things like, "I remember how idealistic I was when I came here—you'll realize the truth soon enough." Remember—work is what you make of it, and you can combat the Chatty Coworker with a few quick comebacks.

* Surprise him with, "I love my job. I'm excited to stay here," even if you're ready to jump ship the first chance you get.
* Agree with him to shut him up. Tell him, "You're so right. Your advice is the best." He doesn't have to know you're secretly cursing him out.
* Be totally honest. Tell him, "I know the road ahead will not be easy but I'm confident I will be successful." In a few years when he's working for you, you can toss in an "I told you so."

The Wise Advisor

While older friends and siblings who have been through it all before can sometimes offer valuable advice, they tend to think that they know how your life is going to turn out based on *their* experiences. They may try to calm your nerves and help you along by saying things like "I only had to do all the filing and faxing for two years before people recognized my talents. Don't worry. The time will go fast for you." You can combat such well-intended but negative advice in several ways.

❋ Remember that they are only trying to help. Good friends don't always say the right thing, but they do try. Thank them for their input and remember not to do the same thing to other people when you're the "wise, older friend."

❋ Change the subject. Try to get some advice you can actually use from the wiser friend, like where in town you can buy the best apartment furnishings or how to resell things you no longer want. If the Wise Advisor is in chatting mode, she'll offer you advice on any topic you bring up. Might as well take advantage of it.

❋ Be honest. Tell friends "I just need to figure things out on my own. That's how I am." Blaming yourself for being unreceptive to advice makes them feel less offended that you aren't taking their words of wisdom seriously.

If you feel that you have both feet planted on solid ground, then the university has failed you.

Robert Gohen

The Bumbling Bureaucrats

Human resources departments, employment agencies, and other official bureaucracies can often be more harmful than helpful to New Graduates. They will often try to pigeonhole you

● enthusiasm rubs off We tend to become like the people we spend the most time with. Spend too much time with the chain-smoking gypsy lady and next thing you know, you'll be sporting beads and a purple embroidered dress with a pack of menthols in the pocket. Always surround yourself with people who support your dreams and share your enthusiasm for life.

into second-rate positions based on your age and youthful look. So if the temp agency worker tells you "We have the perfect job for you. You know how to clean toilets, right?" you can take these smart steps to make it past the gatekeepers.

✳ Showcase your strengths. Make sure your resume does not scream "new kid" by listing your education first and your job experience last. Don't give the Bumbling Bureaucrats any reason to eliminate you from consideration for the good jobs.

✳ Go straight to the top. Write letters to senior managers at companies instead of sending a resume to the HR department or an employment agency. Avoid all communication with the Bumbling Bureaucrats.

✳ Attack on every front. Increase your odds by finding out about job opportunities through every agency, Web site, and acquaintance in town. Don't rely on one person or place to find the right opportunity for you.

The Sensible Senior

The Sensible Senior is that older person who grew up during a different time and views your New Graduate optimism as naiveté, and your enthusiasm as rebelliousness. A Sensible Senior will say things like, "I remember when I was your age and I thought I was going to do all these fabulous things. Oh, to be young again." You can respond in a way that shows respect while still maintaining your sass.

✳ Thank her for lighting the fire. Perhaps the Sensible Senior's words are a good warning urging you to act fast and grab the bull by the horns to make things happen in your life.

✳ Thank her for creating a sense of urgency but remind yourself that times have changed. Remember that she is operating from a difficult focal point.

✳ Evaluate your own level of self-confidence. To achieve a goal, you must believe in it regardless of what people around you say. So if the Sensible Senior's doomsday advice leaves a knot in your stomach, work on building self-confidence so you can't be affected by the pessimistic thoughts of others.

Without education we are in a horrible and deadly danger of taking educated people seriously.

G. K. Chesterton

The Experience Quotient

You might know how to solve Fermat's last theorem but your boss won't even let you distribute an elementary data-entry report to senior management. "You don't have the experience," he claims. You're dying to apply to that dream magazine job but it requires three to five years of experience. You'd love to drive cross-country but skeptical parents and friends say, "Are you sure you can do that by yourself?" During your days as a New Graduate, it can seem that wherever you turn, a voice is yelling "You just aren't experienced enough to do the things you want to do."

This strange barrier is called the Experience Quotient. As a New Graduate, it is your job to laugh at this unusual roadblock and then politely ignore the proclamations of the people who claim you need experience before you can live. There's one

Wizard Work: Brain Surgery and the Like

Strike out into the world and do the things you want to do with enthusiasm, but accept the fact that some tasks truly do require a skilled hand and experienced eye. Here are a few examples of things that should be left to trained professionals.

Separating conjoined twins. Taking a scalpel to a human body requires knowledge and skill. Leave this job to the surgeons!

Assembling cosmetics from raw chemicals. While the idea of creating your own fabulous skin care collection is alluring, it's useful to have some lab training before attempting anything that involves a Bunsen burner.

Cooking dinner at a gourmet restaurant. While you're a whiz with ramen, only an experienced hand should attempt to make a soufflé for paying customers.

Competing in the Olympics. While it's true that a girl can dive into a pool gracefully, she shouldn't expect to win the Olympic gold without doing a few laps at the Y first.

Deciphering the workings of the human mind. Even Freud couldn't figure out what makes some people's brains work the way they do. Only an experienced shrink should try to explain your boss's bizarre behavior.

important thing to remember about the Experience Quotient: It's impossible to get experience without doing what you want to do. So take the road trip, apply for the job, do whatever it is you dream of doing—because you're never going to gain experience without taking chances.

Keep in mind that there are plenty of things you can do without any experience at all. Examine your goals and recognize those things that are Wizard Work (jobs that require a high level of education and skill) and Rookie Work (the things that you can do—even when people think you can't). You'll soon realize that

Rookie Work: Um, Most Things in Life

Aside from the few tasks in life that call for a pro, the New Grad can give just about anything a go. So don't let the Experience Quotient scare you into staying put in a humdrum job. Recognize that many things in life can be performed just fine by a rookie.

Running for public office. It actually seems as if the less experience one has the greater the chances for success. Green = Political Machine.

Starting a profitable small business. If the kid selling Kool-Aid on the street corner can do it, so can any girl who wants to turn a profit.

Drawing, painting, and other creative pursuits. Though education can teach a girl to stay inside the lines, a true artist knows no boundaries. Sometimes too much training can dull raw talent and creativity.

Just about any office task. Though issuing a report or filling out an invoice request can seem intimidating to an inexperienced worker, before long she can complete these tasks in her sleep. "New" does, not equal "challenging."

though some tasks in life do require experience, there are plenty of tasks that require nothing more than your dream of making them happen.

Inside Her Head

The New Graduate must face the external dream slayers and boot them out of her life. But they aren't the only forces that can stop a girl dead in her tracks and prevent her from achieving her goals. Her own internal fears and insecurities have the potential to do the same. Sometimes these self-imposed limitations can be the worst dream slayers of all. The New Graduate must work hard to keep the enthusiasm of her youth alive so she doesn't

If you have made mistakes, even serious ones, there is always another chance for you. What we call failure is not the falling down but the staying down.

Mary Pickford

end up a crazy cat lady counting the days until retirement. But with a little spunk and determination, she can overcome these obstacles and enjoy her life—and so can you.

A Bad Attitude

Once you leave the safe haven of college, you witness the less-than-glamorous ways of the real world firsthand. A friend applies for her dream job and receives the form rejection letter. You trip over the rug and fall flat on your face right when you walk past the hot guy at work. Someone steals your credit card and uses it to buy $3,000 worth of designer knockoff shoes from Asia. It's no wonder your bliss and naiveté are replaced by a cynical real-world perspective.

● reality bites Every day, things happen to challenge your patience. You wake up and stub your toe, the heel breaks off your $300 shoes on your way to work, or your credit card expires ten minutes before you need to make a last-minute birthday gift purchase. Don't let the little annoyances get you down. Remind yourself that these things are just part of life, and then find consolation in knowing that they happen to everyone you know—and best of all, they even happen to those people you don't like.

When faced with the realities of life, it's easy to dismiss your dreams as too daunting to pursue. But the best part of being a New Graduate is your enthusiasm and your energy. These assets will help you overcome any obstacles and keep you reaching for the stars. No matter how many women you are before you're 35, be sure that you keep this part of your New Graduate life with you at all times. Whether you're working at your favorite job or a job you hate, whether you're raising a family or building a handbag empire, keep your spirits high and never stop trying to achieve your goals. Keep connected to the energy and enthusiasm you feel as a girl stepping out into the world for the first time. Allow it to motivate you to live your life with sass at every stage along the way.

While one person hesitates because he feels inferior, the other is busy making mistakes and becoming superior.

— Henry C. Link

Fear of Making a Big Goof

It's easy to hold yourself back because of your fear of making mistakes. With so much to think about every day, it's normal to feel that any decision you make is going to alter your life forever and you'll be on the front page of every tabloid, labeled "The Big Loser." But remember this—you can't move up the ladder of success if you are terrified you're going to slip and land on your head.

● **the first step is the smallest** The journey of 1,000 miles might begin with a single step, but that first step is the hardest to take. The journey gets exponentially easier as you go along.

Minor Mishaps

Some mistakes a girl makes in her life are so insignificant that people forget them moments after they happen. Others are too hilarious to be forgotten:

- She pulls her suitcase by the strap on her business trip because she doesn't realize it has a handle zipped up in the top.
- She pours coffee on her pancakes because she thinks the container holds syrup.
- She feathers her hair for her high school yearbook photo.
- She has a ten-minute phone conversation with someone, hangs up, and has no idea who it was.
- She takes nighttime cold medicine in the morning thinking it will help her nasal drip.
- She flushes her tampons down the toilet in the hotel room, clogs it, and the weird maintenance man has to come dig them out.

All human beings are riddled with imperfections. Just look around at some of the men you've dated! But most mistakes have little if any impact on our lives. Take a few minutes to examine the mistakes people make. You'll feel better once you see that most of them are pretty inconsequential. You'll also be relieved to see that you aren't the only one making them.

The man who graduates today and stops learning tomorrow is uneducated the day after.

Newton D. Baker

Funny Faders

Some of the mistakes the New Graduate makes seem horrendous at the time, but in hindsight they fade and become hysterical blunders she hopes to never commit again.

- She tells her boss about the crappy university her sister attended. She later learns it is his alma mater.
- She uses her birth control pill pack as a bookmark in the corporate library and then accidentally leaves it in the most popular book.
- She walks from the bathroom to her bedroom naked, thinking no one is home, but runs into her beau showing his buddies the new apartment.
- She decides to use hydrogen peroxide to dye her hair bright blond and it turns out orange.
- She has a fit in front of dozens of people at the cash register, insisting she's right about the price, and then she realizes she's wrong after all.

The Fab Future

Sometimes a New Graduate will remember her school days as an idyllic time when life was stress-free. She'll hear people say, "Oh, you're in for it now. Things aren't going to be easy anymore," and their comments will frighten her into thinking her life is over. She'll think about how difficult it will be to say goodbye to summers off, parental support, and instant friends waiting in a dining hall to hang out. But even though she misses things about being a kid as she assimilates into the real world, she also has new opportunities galore to get

Real Life Rocks Because

- You finally have a steady income and can stop collecting soda cans to make an extra buck.
- You can take classes just for fun without stressing out about the grade or whether or not "The History of Fashion" will look weird on your transcript.
- You can tell your mother to stop freaking out about everything you do, even though she probably never will.
- The people you know do not all live in the same building, so you actually have some degree of anonymity.
- You meet lots of new and interesting people.
- You get to drink beer that doesn't taste like it was brewed in a toilet.
- When your workday is done, it's done, and there are no papers or schoolwork dangling over your head.
- Guys finally have to shave their nasty goatees for work.
- You can read trashy literature that is not part of a recommended reading list.
- When you go out at night your feet no longer stick to the floor like they did in the college frat houses.

excited about, a fabulous future that holds so much more than the fickle days of youth.

Celebrate the fab future and look forward to it. As long as you hold on to your dreams and enthusiasm, you will have a future that is worth celebrating.

If I had my life to live over I'd dare to make more mistakes next time.

Nadine Stair

Real-Life Tales from New Graduates

66 I wore a floral skirt and shoes with bows on them to work in New York City. They were really popular in my hometown so I figured they'd carry over. Now I call that outfit my Laura Ingalls gear. 99

66 My mother told me not to try to start my own small business because I need a "real job." It's been ten years and the company is doing great. 99

66 My father said not to buy a keyboard because I would start a fire in my apartment. Do keyboards spontaneously combust? I guess he was afraid I would become a 'music type.' I still play today and I'm not a traveling band groupie. 99

66 I really thought my life was over when I turned 23 because a few of my sister's friends still in college said it sounded so old to them. Looking back, it is hysterical to think that I thought I was old at that age. 99

66 People at my company seemed so impressive when I first started. I still think some of them are, but I was really wrong about others. With each passing month on the job, I gained confidence and started to see people for who they really are. 99

66 I wanted to grow up. I wanted all the dumb cliques and bad boy behavior to end. But part of me was terrified that once it did end, I would miss it . . . and sometimes I do. 99

chapter 2

thedollarlessdiva
cereal, tuna, and a lotta debt

the dollarless diva at a glance

nickname
Credit Card Queen

look
Consistent and unsophisticated, a bit worn.

fashion
Favorite black Gap dress, purchased on sale, worn for five
Fridays in a row.

phrase
"I really can't afford it" or "Got five bucks I can borrow?"

love interest
Any guy who can buy her a meal that is not mac and cheese.

favorite songs
"Material Girl" by Madonna, "She Works Hard for the Money"
by Donna Summer.

events/activities
Outdoor hikes, free museums, trips to the public library, waiting
tables, and other moneymaking side-gigs.

friends
Multiple roommates and the customer service representative
at the student loan servicing center.

life goal
To be able to buy enough clothes to go a full work week
without repeating outfits.

With a degree in hand and a new leather binder holding copies of her resume, the New Graduate is certain she will command a salary that will allow her to live the postgraduation lifestyle she has always dreamed about. Needless to say, she's quite surprised when the best job offer she gets is for a receptionist position that pays a dollar above minimum wage. She tries to look at the bright side: she'll be able to afford bologna and cheese for a while, get lots of exercise from walking everywhere to save cash, and she'll appreciate the finer things in life someday when she can afford them. Until then she is resigned to eating rice and canned soup, wearing the same pair of pants almost every day, and using her credit card to charge gum. She is the Dollarless Diva.

The Dollarless Diva phase is that time in a girl's life when she starts to wonder what she did to deserve the "multiple roommates sleeping in bunk beds" arrangement that's ruining her love life. She buys instant lottery tickets, steals rolls of toilet paper from work, and spends at least ten minutes a day doing the "bring my sandwich" versus "buy my sandwich" savings calculation. Student loan officers stalk her, and her parents complain when she uses their calling card. But she's certain that with a little hard work and some major luck, it won't be long until she'll be able to pull herself out of the discount stores and buy the Dolce & Gabbana jeans she's been eyeing.

This Dollarless Diva stage is one that all women—except maybe Paris Hilton—go through in their lives, but (fortunately) few of us remain in it forever. With a little perspective and a couple of helpful tips (Marry rich? Kill off your old wealthy aunt?), you can learn to laugh a little at your own cashless bank account and live like a queen even on limited means. So if you're a Dollarless Diva right now, read on and breathe a sigh of relief knowing that greener days are ahead. If you're through with this phase, put yourself back in your old worn-down shoes for a minute and remember what it was like to ration peanut butter and reuse paper towels. Take a trip down memory lane and remember this stage as a fabulous experience that changed you for the better, one that made you appreciate real stainless steel eating utensils and $4 iced lattes like nothing else in your life has since.

Life in the Poor Lane

Life in the poor lane is a surreal experience that can drive even the most rational woman to become obsessed with casinos, store-brand everything, Internet clearance sales, and her mother's dry chicken (anything is gourmet if it's not canned tuna). There are three major types of Dollarless Divas living life in the poor lane: (1) the No Money Honey, who can barely make ends meet on

Anyone can be great with money. With money, greatness is not a talent but an obligation. The trick is to be great without money.

Unknown

• never put your money where your mouth is. Don't let the guy you're dating deal with your cash, because you might not be with him forever. Once you break up, there's no way to take back the knowledge he has of your finances. You would have to kill him to keep him quiet.

her tight debt-laden budget; (2) the Undervalued Chick, who makes some cash but not nearly what she's worth; and (3) the Faux-Poor Princess, who complains about being strapped for cash on her weekend trip to Europe. Determine which one of these Dollarless Divas you've been or are right now.

The No Money Honey

The No Money Honey struggles every minute of every day to make ends meet. She's smart, savvy, and completely capable of holding a job, but for now she just can't get her financial situation to net positive. So she borrows from friends, develops innovative ways to earn a buck, and buys everything on sale. The No Money Honey:

* Receives a warm meal of burger and fries paid for by a friend and feels like she's eating at a five-star restaurant.
* Shows up late to every group dinner and has a water so she doesn't have to contribute money.
* Longs to be able to afford a cup of coffee from Starbucks.
* Cuts out coupons and keeps them in a booklet in her handbag.
* Eats the peanuts on the bar during cocktail hour like she's a starving orphan.
* Owns a book that spells out strategies for picking lucky lotto numbers and one that lists nationwide sweepstakes.
* Washes several clothing items in the sink so she doesn't have to pay for Laundromat services as frequently.

✻ Cooks chicken and eats it for a week as chicken soufflé, chicken casserole, chicken parmigiana, chicken noodle soup, chicken cutlet on a roll, chicken stew and, on the seventh day, chicken surprise.

✻ Owns at least one furniture item that she picked out of the garbage and refinished.

✻ Sews funky buttons on her old shirt to make it look like a new purchase.

✻ Drinks before she goes out with friends so she doesn't have to pay bar prices for alcohol.

✻ Attends work parties and weddings and accepts every date solely for the free food.

✻ Stashes chicken wings in her bag on all-you-can-eat wing night.

✻ Cuts her own hair using a three-way mirror.

✻ Thinks the strange metal IKEA "put-it-together-yourself" twisty screwdriver is an actual tool.

Fear strikes the Dollarless Diva's heart when she checks her bank balance. But she isn't destined to remain in the red forever—she has a brighter financial future ahead of her.

I'm poor but I can't figure out what part of my life is suffering. I am ten pounds overweight, so I'm getting enough food. My closet is full of shoes, so my credit cards are working fine. And the candles provide plenty of light at night in the apartment.

Anonymous

The Undervalued Chick

The Undervalued Chick makes enough money to scrape by but she knows she should be making more, so she constantly feels poor. She thinks she's doing okay until she sees her same job at another company listed on the Internet for double the salary. The Undervalued Chick:

* Receives a year-end bonus that, after taxes, is worth just enough to buy groceries for a month.
* Has a job that requires nice clothes but only has enough outfits to make it through one week without repeating.
* Is mistaken for a college intern regularly and is asked to do menial labor.
* Takes direction daily from a boss who has half her ability but receives twice her pay.
* Was educated at an institution where tuition costs more than a house in a chic neighborhood, but currently lives in a shack with three roommates.
* Sits in a cubicle next to her boss's son, who gets paid 20 percent more for doing the same thing she does.
* Has an uncontrollable urge to scream out "I'm too smart for this job" at least once a day.

The Undervalued Chick can move mountains if she's given the chance. But she feels that for now all she can do is wait and hope that a few more wrinkles and a pair of fake wire-rim glasses will give her clout in the future.

I've got all the money I'll ever need, if I die by four o'clock.

Henny Youngman

Stretch Your Dollars

As a true Dollarless Diva, you must make every penny you earn last a long time. You can do this by thinking about the things your great-grandmothers did to save money during the Depression, and then coming up with a few cost-cutters of your own:

- Watering down the orange juice.
- Turning every shampoo and salad dressing bottle upside down to get out every last drop.
- Buying "CVS Tooth Cream" instead of Colgate or Crest.
- Checking out other people's garbage to see if there is anything of use in it
- Buying the cheap, chafing toilet paper.
- Knitting people lovely brightly colored fashionable sweaters for holidays.
- Making ice cream cones from a half gallon instead of buying them from the ice cream truck.
- Purchasing several packages of meat on sale and freezing them for future use.
- Shopping in bulk stores for items like the world's largest and most economical jar of mayo.
- Using paper towels, tissues, saran wrap, and wrapping paper more than once.

The Faux-Poor Princess

The few lucky girls with tons of cash from day one are not immune to feeling like the Dollarless Diva. As much as we find it difficult to feel sorry for them, the reality is that a girl feels poor or rich relative to those people around her. So even if she can afford a $500 dress, she will still feel deprived if her friends spend thousands. It seems messed up, but then life in the faux-poor lane is not exactly normal. The Faux-Poor Princess:

✳ Gets depressed because her best friend bought the new model BMW.

✳ Complains constantly that she's tight on cash but in the next breath talks about her parents' new mansion in Beverly Hills.

✳ Actually buys the clothes created by world-renowned designers that are featured in fashion magazines.

✳ Never has money to chip in for dinner but takes fabulous trips to exotic locations every few months.

✳ Borrows other people's clothes because she's "low on cash."

✳ Feels cheated because her summerhouse didn't come with a Jacuzzi.

✳ Claims she "can't afford her apartment," and then moves into a place with six bedrooms and a pool.

✳ Swears she roughed it in the ghetto growing up.

A Faux-Poor Princess can feel as stressed out as an Undervalued Chick because in her mind, she is really not wealthy enough to fulfill her basic needs—weekly shopping sprees, monthly trips out of the country, and fresh lettuce from the new, trendy gourmet grocery.

Life as a Dollarless Diva in any capacity is characterized by an obsession with money, even for a girl who is ordinarily as selfless as Mother Teresa. It's just difficult to stop thinking about cash when you feel that you never have enough. Luckily, this time in life does not last forever. Even if you don't marry rich or win the lottery, you can leave this phase far behind if you keep in mind a few important principles of personal finance.

● **build credit** Whether you're trying to buy a home or help your kids go to college, some day your credit will be under scrutiny. Always keep your track record clean by paying your credit card bills on time. This credit record tells potential lenders that you are a reliable person. It's really too bad men don't wear their credit report on their forehead.

You can be young without money but you can't be old without it.

Tennessee Williams

The Road to Riches

A Dollarless Diva *can* afford to review a few simple lessons in cash management so she feels reassured that she will always know the right way to handle the green stuff. As confusing as stock symbols and nightmarish investment lingo can be, the way to keep your wealth at its peak position is to follow the very basic "RICH" chick principles:

❋ Rake in the dough
❋ Invest like the best
❋ Cover all debt that has an interest rate attached to it
❋ Have a whole lot of fun too

Any chick who commits these principles to memory will be on the road to riches in no time.

Rake in the Dough

Unfortunately money doesn't fall out of the sky—unless, of course, some girl annoyed with her rich banker boyfriend decides to dump his life savings off a ten-story building. So we have to work for it. To be happy, you don't have to rake in as much dough as Donald Trump but you do need to determine what your own personal goals are and how you're going to achieve them. You might want to teach, run for office, make a living in the arts, work on Wall Street, or become a full-time mom. Whatever you choose, recognize the tradeoffs and make sure you're happy with the work/life mix you pick. Keep a few things in mind, whether you're about to interview for your first job or you're making a career switch.

Know What to Expect

Don't choose a job based on what you see on television or what friends say about a certain profession. Very few careers mimic those portrayed in a prime-time drama. So instead of guessing what your life will be like as a doctor or business-woman, ask experienced people in that field what to expect. Seek out answers to key questions such as: What can I expect my salary to be? What is the day-to-day work like? What will my hours be? How fast can I expect to move up? Know the answers to these questions so you can make an educated decision.

*I've been rich and I've been poor.
Believe me, honey, rich is better.*

Sophie Tucker

Understand Demand

Read job listings so you know what skills are in demand in the market and what kind of cash they translate into. If guys aren't into bold feminine fashion this season, even the smart-est, most skilled designer of Capri pants for men will not make money. Educate yourself so you can make an informed career choice and get what you want out of the work you do.

Avoid a Stifling Workplace

You might be capable of running your own company, but if the human resources bureaucracy only promotes one person each decade, your talent will go unnoticed. If this is the case,

● money tip No matter which career you choose, do your best and make it a habit to ask for a raise regularly (allude to secret tapes of your boss surfing porn sites if necessary).

get the heck out of there. Never stick around just because you're comfortable in a position. Move to an environment that rewards your skills and gives you opportunity to grow.

Do What You Like

The more you like what you're doing, the better you'll be at it. Try to find a job that you enjoy for some reason. Though no job is perfect (and most don't even come close), search for a job that has one small enjoyable nugget somewhere in it, even if it's just the free coffee. It will make your days more bearable.

Very few of us start out in the world with a six-figure salary and a posh apartment, but just because you're dying for cash doesn't mean you should settle for the first job someone tosses your way. Establish your own personal game plan and follow through with it. Don't allow anyone to pressure you into taking a job in a field that doesn't feel right in your gut. You are the one who has to live your life every day, so make sure you're happy with the choices you make. Once you identify the plan that's right for you, pursue it wholeheartedly. Then, whether you're raking in dough or you're a full-time mom with a baby in tow, you will be happy. Ultimately, that's what being rich really means.

Invest Like the Best

The word "invest" can be scary because it conjures images of lots of numbers, strange ticker symbols, and men and women wearing suits and glasses seated around a conference table. But regardless of how much money you make, it is important to get comfortable with investing. You might think, "This topic is so

● shop & save A pair of pants purchased half-off cancels out the purchase of a full-price top, just as diet soda cancels out a chocolate chip cookie. So shop away.

boring. I'm still collecting the deposits on bottles to make ends meet. I have nothing extra to invest," but you do. Even if it's a dollar a day, investing is crucial for any girl who wants to get out of the Dollarless Diva phase for good. Financial experts can skip this section, but if you are frightened to death by e-mails about your 401(k), read on.

"It takes money to make money" may be a cliché, but it's also the truth. If you have money and invest it wisely, it will grow exponentially over the years. Of course, if you buy cute shoes with your cash you'll have them today, and that's pretty satisfying too—more on carpe diem later. Let's assume that you want to invest your money instead. The key is to find a place to put it where it will earn the most interest at a level of risk that you can tolerate. Though the concept of interest is not intuitive when we start out in the world, once you understand it, you will have the power to ditch the Dollarless Diva days faster than you can scream "Hand over your wallet, rich bitch!" in a dark alley.

Companies and organizations of all types need cash to operate, so they "borrow" yours and promise to give you interest

Money, says the proverb, makes money. When you have got a little, it is often easy to get more. The great difficulty is to get that little.

Adam Smith

(i.e., a little extra) in return for the "loan." These are a few common investments that will earn interest for you:

Stocks

Stocks give you ownership in a company. When you put your money in a stock, you own a piece of that company. The good news is that if the company does well, the piece you own is more valuable and you're not a Dollarless Diva anymore. But if the company tanks, your piece of the company loses value. That means goodbye filet mignon and hello tuna. Stocks are considered riskier investments.

Bonds

Not at all like James Bond, given they are neither cute nor savvy. When you purchase a bond, you're making a loan to the entity issuing it. That entity then uses your cash and pays you interest in return. Unlike stocks, bonds are not shares of ownership. Bonds are issued for a specific period of time at a specific interest rate. Therefore they are, on the average, a bit safer than stocks.

Mutual Fund

This is a portfolio of stocks and bonds you can invest in. A mutual fund "spreads risk," which means that the success of the fund is not dependent on any one company or bond issuer, but instead on how the collection fares as a whole. This investment is generally a safe bet for small investors who don't have much knowledge of individual stock or bond performance.

Checking or Savings Account

You earn only a measly amount of interest when you put your money in a bank account. Bank accounts are intended for cash that you will need in the short-term for a manicure and a martini.

The Coffee Equation

1. Figure out how much you spend on coffee each year. For example, if you spend $1.50 on an extra-large coffee every day, multiply it by 365 days in a year and you can see that you spend $547.50 annually on your morning brew.

2. As a savin' maven, you might decide to forgo this cup of coffee and save the $1.50 instead. Assuming you can earn 10 percent interest each year on this savings, in 25 years you will have $5,393 ... but you'll also be very sleepy and irritated with the world.

3. You decide: is it worth it? Would you rather have a cup of coffee every day for the next year? Or an extra $5,000 when you're nearing retirement? Go for the cup of joe and instead spend some extra time talking your rich aunt into writing that $5,000 for you into her will.

Most likely a couple of thousand dollars extra in twenty-five years will not be worth forgoing an entire lifetime of that creamy caffeinated beverage. Consider other possible windfalls between now and then—marrying rich, winning the lottery, being discovered by a designer and turned into the next hot runway model. Go ahead and drink away!

Money Market Fund

A money market is like a bond, but the period of time you hold it for is shorter. Because you get your money back much faster, the interest rate is lower. (The longer you're willing to "loan" your money to an entity, the more it will offer you in interest). Money markets are a good place to put extra cash that you'll need soon because you can get it out quickly and you'll earn slightly more than you would if you put it in a checking or savings account.

CD

Not just a disk with music on it anymore! "CD" in the world of finance stands for certificate of deposit. You can purchase one

*Beware of little expenses. A small
leak will sink a great ship.*

Benjamin Franklin

at your bank, which will hold on to your money for a specified period of time and give you interest in return. This type of investment is very safe but the interest is usually not high.

401(k)

A 401(k) allows you to put money into an account straight out of your paycheck before taxes are subtracted, so you get to invest money without paying taxes on it first. Your employer usually matches some part of what you put in. Then the entire sum is invested for you by an organization your company has elected to use. Your money stays in the 401(k) until you retire. Investing this way allows you to build up a nice sum for later in life with the help of your employer. It also enables you to earn money on income that would otherwise be taxed. The government will tax the 401(k) when you finally do draw upon it, but until then, you earn tax-free interest on the entire sum.

● **the power of interest** Punch a number into a calculator—for instance, $100. Multiply it by 1.07, which adds 7 percent. You get $107.00, which is the amount you'll have after the first year of investment at an interest rate of 7 percent. Next year you'll earn another 7 percent; however, instead of earning it on only $100, you'll earn it on $107. Your new total will be $114.49. Each year you are earning money on a larger amount, so your money will grow exponentially. Compounded interest will cause your money to grow faster than you can find a rich old husband with a terminal illness (but that shouldn't stop you from trying.)

Annoying Younger Sibling

If you have a sibling who always asks you for money, you can tag on a little interest. After all, what are sisters for?

These basic investment vehicles are ways any Dollarless Diva can pull herself out of the state of financial ruin, otherwise known as the years following college graduation. When you first start out in the world, your investment strategy will probably be to stick as much as possible in your 401(k). Then if you can, you might start putting a little in stocks or bonds. Before you make any move with your money, seek out the advice of a brilliant banker type, preferably a cute guy who can explain it all to you in detail over cocktails and dinner.

Cover All Debt That Has an Interest Rate Attached to It

Remember the days when "C" was for cookie? These days it stands for "Cover all debt that has an interest rate attached to it." Just as you earn interest when you loan out your cash, other people charge you interest when they loan you money. The biggest culprits are credit card companies and student loan officers. You'll grasp this concept quickly if you're stalked by Master-Card, Visa, or Sallie Mae. To get yourself out of this nightmare cycle of credit card debt, you have to work hard to pay back more each month on your debt than the interest they charge you. Every moment that you have outstanding debt with an

● an important rule If the interest rate on your debt is higher than the interest you can earn through an investment, focus on paying off your debt. If, however, you can earn 5 percent interest through an investment and your student loans only require you to pay 2 percent interest, change your strategy. Make a monthly payment on your loans that's greater than the interest accumulated that month, but don't go overboard and pay off the entire debt. You will be wealthier in the long run if you put your extra cash where it can earn higher interest, and pay off the debt slowly.

interest rate attached to it, you are losing cash. When you pay back more than the interest and cut into the principal amount you owe, you slowly chisel down the debt. The annoying little sucker will eventually be gone!

Whoever said money can't buy happiness simply didn't know where to go shopping.

Bo Derek

Have a Whole Lot of Fun Too

Pay your bills on time, invest a little bit each month, and generally be responsible about money, but don't scrape by day to day while a big fat wad of cash sits in your bank account. No way! Head for the Bahamas, Diva.

As a general rule, no girl should deprive herself of happiness in order to save money. If you make an effort to put something away out of each paycheck, you can then allow yourself to enjoy the rest of your cash now. Sometimes sacrificing a pleasure today is just not worth the dollar or two it saves in the long run.

Creative Cash

At this point you're probably thinking, "Okay, great, but this investment stuff is long-term and I need cash now. My kitchen table is from my aunt's old apartment. My bed is a donation from my sister. My mom gave me her dishes. I just want one item I purchased on my own, something I didn't get from a garage sale. What do I do?"

If you need cash quickly so you can stop putting water in the soap dispenser to make the suds last longer, read on. While there are no legitimate schemes that will make $1 million overnight, there are plenty of ways to make an extra buck or two today. So ditch the lottery fantasy for now (but keep buying a ticket once in a while just in case your lucky day comes), and think realistically about short-term strategies for acquiring cash . . . legally of course.

Professional Shopper

When you're chowing down cold cereal for dinner on a Saturday night, the Anna Nicole Smith method of making money (marry a rich, sickly old man) might seem really appealing. But why not opt for a more noble alternative, like getting part-time work as a shopper for the elderly, or doing some other job for an older person that only takes a few hours a week. Think of how much more appealing your love life will be, too, when you can just work for that rich old guy instead of marrying him.

Part of the $10 million I spent on gambling, part on booze and part on women. The rest I spent foolishly.

George Raft

Part-Time Waitress

When you're sneaking food into the movie theater because you can't afford the snack bar markup, you might feel an urge to hit the casinos and play the slots until your lucky pull comes. But if you're aching for cash that badly, why not take your passion for entertainment elsewhere and work part-time as a waitress in a fun bar or restaurant? Lots of places hire for only a few

● trial by fire   You won't get out and stay out of the Dollarless Diva stage by avoiding tasks that seem daunting. So jump in headfirst and figure out how to read the numbers on your health insurance card, register for your 401(k), or put a little money in any of the investments explained in this chapter. Just as we all learn to put on a bra despite how scary the hooks in the back seem at first peek, we also learn many other things in life simply by giving them a try.

hours a week and if you keep it fun and light, it will seem more like an opportunity to meet new people than it will a job.

Teenager Tutor

When the heels on your shoes are worn into the ground and you see a teenager wearing Prada pumps, you might want to slap her silly and take her wad of cash—and the shoes too. But why not consider tutoring these kids part-time and making an extra buck that way?

Pet Sitter

When you walk by the gym and you can't join because the fee is so outrageous, you might consider getting in a good workout by snagging an old lady's purse and making a run for it. But why not become a paid dog walker and get your exercise and your cash that way?

He who knows how to be poor knows everything.

Jules Michelet

Entrepreneuer

If you've studied your knockoff Kate Spade closely enough to know how every thread compares to your coworker's real one, you might have thought about selling fake designer goods online. But why not clean out your own apartment (and your sibling's house and your parents' house) and sell all that stuff on an online auction site? You never know what you might make off your old Strawberry Shortcake dolls or that funky '70s jacket your mom wore during her hippie phase.

My father told me that if you saw a man in a Rolls Royce you could be sure he was not a gentleman unless he was the chauffeur.

Earl of Arran

Caterer

If you hear a girl say she's having her wedding reception at a fancy hotel but you're certain yours will be at the Motel 6, you might feel tempted to crash her affair and raid the gift table. But why not think about working for a catering company on an event-by-event basis so you can make cash from these fancy receptions in your spare time?

Even though quick fixes like these won't leave you jumping for joy in piles of the green stuff, they will give you a few extra bucks for the moment. Eventually, if you keep your nose to the grindstone, work hard, save, and invest, you will pull yourself out of the Dollarless Diva stage for good and you won't need creative cash anymore. Your days of praying for that inheritance from your rich old aunt will be far behind and you'll feel in control of your own financial destiny.

Signs You're on the Road to Riches

It can take a while to build up a nice nest egg, but once you do, you'll start to notice that you just aren't as cost-conscious as you used to be. You'll know you're on the road to riches when:

- You actually buy the shower gift off the registry instead of trying to find a cheaper present that looks expensive.

- You purchase a pair of pink polka dot shoes because you want them and not because they'll go with every outfit you own for the next five years.

- You take a cab home right up to your door instead of stopping five blocks away to save the extra dollar.

- You remember sticking your fingers together almost permanently with rubber cement while attempting to wallpaper your bathroom, so you opt to hire a professional to do the house renovations.

- You've been in the same stores in the mall so many days in a row that security thinks you're part of a very aggressive shoplifting ring, when actually you're just spending your cash.

- You buy the curtains you want even though they are a few dollars more instead of buying two sets of the cheaper ones and layering them to keep out the light.

- You no longer feel terror in your heart when you've finished a meal at a good restaurant and the bill is brought to the table, and you also don't feel utter relief when someone else picks up the tab. Gratitude and deep appreciation, maybe, but not utter relief.

- When you get invited to the wedding 3,000 miles away, driving doesn't even cross your mind.

- You shop regularly at the stores where all the clothes are arranged neatly on the shelves (even though you still rummage through discount racks on occasion!).

The Spare Change Challenge

You will eventually leave your Dollarless Diva days far behind, and life on a shoestring will become a distant memory. But even when you are finally a true tycoon, you're charged with a responsibility: to remember the lessons you learned when you were struggling to make ends meet. Recall what it felt like to drive the clunky rust-covered car and steal free sandwiches from work meetings to eat later for dinner. These experiences make us nicer, more down-to-earth, and more appreciative of all the good things in life. It would be a bitchy shame if we forgot these lessons and became clueless wenches buying up Prada bags like they're plastic just because we have a few dollars to spare.

A wise man should have money in his head, but not in his heart.

Jonathan Swift

So when you finally leave the Dollarless Diva stage behind, enjoy living in a way that makes you happy and comfortable. Don't be afraid to take pride in your accomplishments and enjoy yourself—you earned it. But don't forget what it was like to struggle a little too. Never turn your nose up at a dollar store or the people who love to shop there and don't pass up the chance to make life a little easier for the Dollarless Divas you know by picking up that tab!

As you move beyond your Dollarless Diva days, keep in mind a few important principles that will help you achieve a balance between spending and saving.

Ditch the Poverty Mentality

Being strapped for cash for too long can condition you to save every penny and think about money incessantly. If you've considered making your toddler pay rent or you've tried to find your dog a part-time job, make a conscious effort to leave this poverty mentality behind. Don't let your days of going without make you obsessed with every penny. Lavish yourself with trips to the spa and fine dining on occasion, and don't hold back when someone needs to borrow a dollar or two. Remember that at one time, that was you.

Money can't buy you happiness but it does bring you a more pleasant form of misery.

Spike Milligan

Use Your "License to Shop" Wisely

It's easy to get used to having things your own way when you have money to spare. But as a former Dollarless Diva, remember that just because you can afford something doesn't mean you have to have it. That's not to say you can't buy a great pair of shoes on sale, but don't blow every penny on that fuchsia Porsche just because the neighbors next door have one.

Cash Is King ... But It's Not Everything

Striving for a monetary goal can give a girl a sense of purpose, but remember to prioritize nonmonetary goals too. Getting a Ph.D., volunteering for a cause, or taking care of the people you love are just as rewarding, if not more so, than hearing cha-ching.

So enjoy your wealth, but at the same time remember what it was like to go without so you always appreciate what you have. Leave your Dollarless Diva days far behind, but not the lessons you learned while living them.

The Dollarless Diva stage is filled with trying times, like those moments when you're invited to the cool party but you relate more to the bathroom attendant than you do to the host, and those nights when you dine on tuna and rye while writing out checks to Sallie Mae. Just continue to work hard and keep your financial wits about you. Soon you will move on to a place in your life where you'll feel secure in your finances and in control of your destiny. As challenging as the Dollarless Diva days are when you're in them, you'll recall them fondly years later and laugh at just how resourceful you could be when you were called upon to stretch your paycheck. Never again in life will you appreciate a free drink, a 10 percent discount, or a ninety-nine-cent store as much as you did when you were a Dollarless Diva. It is a unique time in a girl's life, one to remember and celebrate.

Real-Life Tales from Dollarless Divas

❝I used my parents' calling card to call a friend from a pay phone because I didn't want to use up my cell phone minutes.❞

❝I bought a slightly imperfect dress for $10 and tried to fix it. It ended up being a slightly imperfect $10 cleaning rag.❞

❝I filled my purse with sugar packets from work and brought them home to use in my own kitchen.❞

❝I took all my cash out for the week on Sunday night and separated it into seven amounts so I would know exactly how much I could afford to spend each day.❞

❝I lied about my Payless shoes and said they were Prada. My friends went looking for them and I lied again, insisting they were probably sold out.❞

❝ I refused to take a cab at three in the morning and my friend and I ended up in a dingy neighborhood, all because I was cheap and made us take a train we never took before. ❞

❝ I wanted to win a drawing for a new DVD player so badly that I snuck the entire stack of blank tickets into my bag, filled them all out at home, and went back and put them in. And I won! ❞

❝ I was afraid to answer the door at night because my neighborhood was so sketchy! Turned out, it was two firemen banging on the door because the basement boiler exploded. ❞

theworker**bee**
i can do it all, baby

the worker bee at a glance

nickname
Superwoman, "Type A" Chick, Workaholic

look
Conservative, practical, nothing too flashy; no time for frills.

fashion
A pantsuit, or Ann Taylor skirt and blouse.

phrase
"I'll do it" or "I can stay tonight. No problem."

love interest
The associate she spends long nights with at the conference table.

favorite songs
Classical music (she read that listening to Mozart increases brain power).

events/activities
Work, work, and more work.

friends
Other overachievers who are happy to communicate via instant messaging and understand that she just can't leave the office before 8 P.M.

life goal
To accomplish every task, on time, perfectly.

Dollarless Diva knows that if she's going to make a buck or two and pull herself out of the financial doldrums, she has to work hard. So when she finally lands a job with some potential to move upward, she takes diligence to a new level, offering to hand-scribe the memo if the copy machine is down and inhaling cups of coffee so she has the energy to keep going. With a world of opportunity before her, she sets her sights on the big promotion and decides she's going to do whatever it takes to get there. She becomes the eager, enthusiastic, and dedicated Worker Bee.

The Worker Bee phase is that time in a woman's life when she learns to hold on to a level of responsibility critical for success while also saying "to hell with everything" on occasion. But she doesn't learn this lesson of balance overnight. It only comes after many days of drudgery, weekends staring at a computer screen, and several missed vacations. Only after she pushes herself to the

Confidence is contagious. So is lack of confidence.

Vince Lombardi

limit repeatedly does she realize she can't live like a workaholic maniac forever. Then she takes steps to improve her quality of life. But until she comes to this realization, she works hard, plays rarely, and carries the weight of responsibility on her shoulders.

Superwoman in Action

The Worker Bee is a favorite team member in the office because she's diligent and reliable. She gets the job done quickly, flawlessly, and with enthusiasm, and this energy spills over into other parts of her life. She manages a big project, runs a marathon, organizes a hunger drive, and talks a friend through a tough breakup all in the same week. She is Superwoman, or at least close to it.

If you've been a Worker Bee in your past or you are now, you know that being one is no field day. The urge to do everything well can drive a girl to stay awake around the clock for weeks on end even if she's battling pneumonia. When you're in Worker Bee mode, you'll do whatever you can to check off the duties on your enormous task list, even if getting things done comes at the expense of your health and sanity.

While being diligent and responsible are respectable attributes, a Worker Bee takes her need to achieve one step too far, pushing herself to the limit every day. Review the following characteristics of the Worker Bee to determine if you share any of her habits and needs.

The Worker Bee Is Just a Tad Bit Too Diligent

She makes it through the entire day without going to the bathroom because she doesn't have time to leave her desk. She worries she's not getting her work done fast enough so she stays late and arrives early. She is on a first-name basis with the night-shift security guards and cleaning people at her office.

The Worker Bee Is Afraid to Take Time Off

She hasn't taken a day off in months. She's afraid to miss a moment. In fact, she feels guilty if she takes an extra five minutes for lunch. Even if she's coughing up a lung, you can find her at her desk, sleeves rolled up, working away.

The Worker Bee Helps Anyone Who Asks

She is an employer's dream, saying yes to every project that comes across her desk. She even volunteers to enter the office lottery pool numbers into a spreadsheet, all 300 sets, and she organizes the company outing too.

The Worker Bee Wants to Do Everything Perfectly

She calls herself an idiot if she puts the wrong date on the top of a report. Her headings are centered, her documents spell-checked, and her cost reports in on time. She keeps her files organized and her recycling bin emptied. Meanwhile, her own apartment is a disaster because she is never there. She spends her waking hours at the office.

The Worker Bee Looks Worn Out

She forgets to eat because she's so busy, or eats too much junk trying to find the energy to keep going. Thoughts of everything she needs to do swirl in her brain and make it impossible for her to fall asleep at night. She purchases all her clothes online because she never gets out of work before the stores close. She has no time to take care of herself.

● **go all the way girl** Remember that as a Worker Bee, your idea of balance is probably not exactly normal. For a while, say to yourself, "I'm going to make every effort to relax." Go a little overboard in taking it easy if need be. Only by pushing yourself too far the other way will you actually end up in the middle ground.

The Worker Bee Likes Structure and Control

Her routine drives her every move, day in and day out. When unexpected things happen, they throw her for a loop. She prefers to work from her list and keep to a schedule. If she has to cancel a meeting or do an unexpected task, she feels out of whack for a while. She gets stressed out easily when she doesn't have control over her day.

Thinking is the hardest work there is, which is probably the reason why so few engage in it.

Henry Ford

The Worker Bee Spreads Herself Too Thin

She does her work well but sometimes she wonders if she could do something really spectacular if she had more time. She feels like a workhorse instead of a star. She's a "Jane of all trades," spreading herself too thin at the expense of doing one or two things really well.

The Worker Bee Knows She Needs a Change

She isn't oblivious to the fact that she's working herself to the bone. She's overwhelmed and it's not because her social calendar is too full. She never feels that she has her life under control. In her gut, she knows she needs a break or she's going to go bonkers.

Be honest—do any of those characteristics sound familiar? If you say "I'll do it" more often than you say "I'll take a martini," you might be a Worker Bee. If you take along your leather binder when you do finally take a vacation and think success in life is directly proportional to the crinkles in your forehead, you might be putting too much stock in your ability to get the job done. A Worker Bee pushes and pushes toward her goal with all her energy, time, and enthusiasm, even when she's overwhelmed and exhausted. She takes working hard one step too far. If this sounds like you, read on.

You cannot be anything if you want to be everything.

Solomon Schechter

One Step Too Far

What's wrong with being a hard worker? Didn't Chapter 2 say you have to put your nose to the grindstone to get ahead? While it's true that being a hard worker is a commendable quality, the Worker Bee takes diligence to the extreme, and her hard work actually begins to detract from her progress.

Doing well on the job is more like making a gourmet dish than it is winning a race. In a race, the winner is the one who pushes ahead the hardest and fastest. The success of a dish, however, is more about finding the optimal mix of ingredients than it is about exerting endless effort. Putting in more spices doesn't make the dish better. In fact, it can ruin it. However, no spices at all make the dish bland. The key is to put in just enough without going too far. The same is true when it comes to success on the job. Being too much of a workaholic can actually work against you.

Working Smart

The Worker Bee's diligence undermines her progress because she works hard at the expense of working smart. Working smart means setting priorities so you don't get bogged down in the day-to-day details that don't matter.

● **the airtight alibi** Need a break from work for a day? Try the number one excuse that can get you out of any meeting or task: "I have a doctor's appointment to deal with a highly contagious rash." No one will question your need to flee the office.

A Worker Bee takes on every task that comes her way, even if it's busywork that doesn't contribute to the bottom line. She's so busy with alphabetizing files from forty years ago that she doesn't have time to focus on meaty projects that will get her noticed today. Working smart is more important than working hard. Effort is no good if it doesn't translate into a real impact on the company's success.

People who work sitting down get paid more than people who work standing up.

Ogden Nash

Insecurity

The Worker Bee's diligence works against her because it leaves her feeling insecure and inadequate instead of confident and capable. The harder she tries to accomplish unrealistic goals, the further she falls short. She soon realizes that she just cannot do all the things she wants to do perfectly. She has to let some things go and make others priorities. When she finally does let something slide, she judges herself harshly and feels guilty because she's not Superwoman.

Respect

The Worker Bee's diligence undermines her success because others assume she doesn't have control over her life. At first she

When you are content to be simply yourself and don't compare or compete, everybody will respect you.

Lao Tzu

comes off as someone who simply cares a lot about what she's doing, but as her coworkers get to know her, she seems frazzled. She scrambles to get things done, and takes on more tasks than she needs to instead of sticking to priorities. She doesn't trust and respect herself, which makes it difficult for other people to trust and respect her.

Lazy Guy Enabler

Coworkers begin to view the Worker Bee as the one who will do all the things no one else wants to do. Even other diligent people feel a need to slack on occasion. They know they can push their tasks onto her and she'll get them done. By failing to put her foot down and set boundaries, she becomes a dumping ground for menial projects. This added burden compels her to work harder, and she drives herself deeper into a rut.

Work Atmosphere

The Worker Bee begins to resent people who don't work as hard as she does. She feels angry because she's the one slaving

too tired to tango? Try to fall asleep faster at night by banishing all thoughts about what you need to do the next day. Visualize yourself in a lawn chair on the beach, margarita in hand. Or picture yourself sitting on a tire swing on a breezy summer day. Focus on these peaceful images and you'll be dreaming before you know it.

away while others are enjoying their lives, taking vacation time, and eating lunch. Sometimes she makes the atmosphere tense for those who want to live a more balanced life, and this angst in the workplace detracts from team performance.

The Big Picture

The Worker Bee is so caught up in detail that she sometimes fails to see how her work is contributing to the bigger picture. An employee who excels not only does her job but also looks for opportunities beyond her day-to-day work to make the company better. An all-star employee contributes to the company's overall mission and success. The Worker Bee often lacks this big-picture perspective because the daily grind keeps her from looking up, taking a breath, and noticing the world around her.

Successful people are the ones who think up things for the rest of the world to keep busy at.

Don Marquis

Not Enough Fun, Friends, and Frou-Frou Drinks

The Worker Bee's hard work prevents her from having fun in her life. She ignores the fact that people actually do better on the job if they take time away from it on occasion. She skips birthdays and holidays, and even misses weddings and funerals to put in extra hours at the office. She toils away at the expense of her social life, friends, family, and sanity. In the end, this "all work and no play" mentality takes a toll on her performance.

The Worker Bee has many admirable qualities, but she takes working hard a bit too far. This "I can do it all" attitude actually undermines her progress. It leaves her feeling tired, walked on, overburdened, and undercompensated. Others look at her and see a weary coworker who doesn't have her life under control.

● **the achievement buzz** Work can be as addicting as caffeine, alcohol, or nicotine. If you feel a weird sense of exhilaration when you achieve something but you feel down the rest of the time, you might be an achievement addict. When your need to achieve is driving you whacko and a few cocktails won't cure you, seek professional help so you can enjoy your life.

Eventually she realizes she has to find balance and move on from her Worker Bee phase to a more productive, enjoyable place. She starts to think about what balance in her life really means.

From Bonkers to Balance

Obviously too much rest and relaxation won't pay the bills or leave a girl feeling fulfilled for long. There's something to be said for hard work, dedication, and accomplishment. But at the same time, being Superwoman isn't really fulfilling either. You cannot be all things to all people without going a bit nutty. The key is to find a middle ground.

Even after a Worker Bee realizes she needs a change, she doesn't always know exactly how to go about it. After struggling to do a good job for so long, her concept of balance is a bit twisted. She thinks taking five minutes to paint her nails is extravagant, when what she really needs is five weeks off.

Don't tell me how hard you work. Tell me how much you get done.

James J. Ling

Diligent or Doormat?

Sometimes insecurity drives a girl to work extra hard to get ahead. She is new to her job or the work force, so she doesn't yet know where she stands amidst her peers. Most of the time this insecurity is temporary, and it disappears as she acquires experience. But sometimes it doesn't, because she is a "Good Girl" at heart.

A Good Girl works hard because she feels insecure, and that insecurity is prevalent in all parts of her life. It never goes away unless she takes active steps to build her confidence. Good Girl tendencies include things like these:

- She lets the nice old doorman smack her on the ass when she walks into her building because she doesn't want to cause a stir by telling him to knock it off.

- She's afraid to mention to the cashier that he overcharged her because she doesn't want to hold up the line.

- A man slams into her on the street and she responds with "Oh my gosh! I'm so sorry" and then meekly goes on her way.

- Her boyfriend doesn't show up to take her out to dinner as he said he would, and she assumes it's somehow her fault.

- Someone at work yells at her and she goes home crying.

A Good Girl is a pleaser. She wants to make everyone happy, do a good job, and make as few waves as possible. She has a far bigger task ahead of her than the girl who is just insecure because she's new on the job. A Good Girl must increase her confidence in every part of her life before she will be able to ditch her workaholic tendencies. Once she pulls herself out of Good Girl mode, she will stop being a Worker Bee too.

Whether you're a Worker Bee yourself or you're trying to help a friend ditch this phase, take time to think about what balance really means so you know what you're aiming to achieve. In this day and age, when there's so much emphasis on performance, it's easy to be caught up in a rat race and let life pass you by. You can convince yourself that pushing the snooze button in the morning means you're living a balanced lifestyle. But balance means more than a five-minute snooze or a bathroom break here and there.

Balance is NOT:

* Getting to the bed-and-breakfast, setting up your computer immediately, and throwing a tantrum because there's no Internet connection.
* Structuring your workday so you leave just in time to have a chat with your significant other before he goes to bed.
* Taking the assignment to a more thorough level by reading every relevant book in the Library of Congress to support your claims.
* Trying to finish the financial report between cake and ice cream at your toddler's birthday party.
* Reporting to work despite having tuberculosis.
* Overanalyzing your presentation after the fact and trying to gauge how you did by the expression on your boss's face.
* Making yourself sick with worry the night before your employee review.
* Scheduling a day to do nothing. (Shouldn't it just happen naturally?)
* Cursing out a coworker for taking the day off.
* Reviewing an underling's work with a magnifying glass in search of errors.
* Approaching a shopping trip as if it's a project and feeling guilty when you don't hit all the stores in your plan.
* Enforcing your regimen on those around you and getting angry when they think you're nuts.

If you go through a lot of hammers each month, I don't think it necessarily means you're a hard worker. It may just mean that you have a lot to learn about proper hammer maintenance.

Jack Handey

On the flip side, balance IS:

* Taking time to go out with friends on occasion so they don't file a missing persons report.
* Having fun today instead of waiting for the time when all of your work is done.
* Letting go of control and the fear that underlings will mess things up.
* Speaking up when you have too much to do so people don't expect the world of you.
* Rewarding yourself for what you've accomplished instead of feeling bad that there's one remaining task on your list that you didn't get done.
* Encouraging coworkers and underlings to take their vacation time and to make time for their personal lives.
* Setting priorities and sticking to them so the day-to-day grind doesn't get in the way of more important tasks.
* Feeling happy for other people who get promoted instead of feeling terrified that it means they are smarter than you.
* Leaving early when you need to without feeling as if you need to duck out wearing a disguise.
* Having confidence in your work even if you make a mistake once in a while.

✳ Taking five minutes to relax even when you're busy.
✳ Realizing that unless a task means life or death, it's really not that important.

Somewhere in the middle of beach bum and bonkers is balance. While balance means different things to different people, it clearly excludes working eighteen-hour days or taking your computer with you when you go on vacation. You can define balance for yourself, but make sure that your concept of personal power includes more than a hot shower. Take ample time to enjoy your life and leave your Worker Bee phase behind for good.

I need to take an emotional breath, step back and remind myself who's actually in charge of my life.

Judith Knowlton

Regaining Control

You know that working hard is important, but working too hard will actually undermine your success and happiness. You need balance. But just how does a girl reach this middle ground when there's so much to do every day? You can start by getting away from it all for a while, taking a much-needed vacation or simply turning off the lights and hiding in bed for a couple of days. But in the end you'll have to return to work, and if you don't have a plan for reducing the stress in your everyday life, you'll fall right back into your Worker Bee routine. What you need is a plan you can follow to achieve balance even when you're back in your frenzied office, where your phone is ringing, your inbox is full, and projects are hanging over your head.

• coffee with coworkers Always schedule time to grab lunch or a cup of coffee with a coworker. It provides a nice, relaxing moment during the day that you don't have to feel guilty about. You can expense it, too, because technically you're discussing work, right?

Taking a Time-Out

Commit to memory these ten workplace tips, which you can apply on the job every day. They will help you ditch the madness of the Worker Bee phase for good and have a more relaxed state of mind all the time, even when life is hectic.

TEN TIPS FOR WORKPLACE SANITY

1. Find the Easy Way Every Day

These words are scary to the Worker Bee. They sound strangely like the philosophy of the bad kid who sat in the back row in high school and never did his homework. But the Worker Bee needs to take a clue from this lazy guy and apply a little bit of his philosophy to her own life.

Too often a Worker Bee dives in and tackles a task with all her energy. She doesn't assess the situation first to determine the easiest, fastest way to get the job done without compromising the end result. If your boss says "Find a few statistics," that doesn't mean "Locate a set of encyclopedias, read them cover to cover, and use regression analysis to analyze the results." Find out exactly what you need to do and determine the easiest way to do it so you never overwork and overstress about a task.

2. Give "No" a Go

The Worker Bee thinks if she says "no" to a project, people will think she's lazy and the world will crumble. Sometimes this inability to say "no" carries over into other parts of her life too. She's everyone's first pick. Her sister calls her if she needs a babysitter, the local charity contacts her to run a bake sale, and friends dump their problems her way. They know she'll take on any task and do it well.

If you have problems saying "no," give it a go for a change and see what happens. If you feel more comfortable providing an excuse to justify saying "no," don't hesitate to tell a little white lie. You don't have to be honest all the time when your sanity is at stake. You'll find that the more often you say "no," the easier it gets, and people do listen. You'll find that the world won't fall apart, and soon you'll wish you'd been saying no all along. Not to mention, you'll have a lot more time and energy for the things you do take on and you'll perform better.

Saying no can be the ultimate self-care.

Claudia Black

3. Mimic the One Who Works and Has Fun

The hardest thing for the Worker Bee to realize is that she will actually do better on the job if she learns to give herself a break once in a while. To get yourself over this "I'll end up labeled a loser if I slack" mentality, find a role model who has achieved balance in her life. This person should be one who is successful and respected, but one who also takes time for her family and knows how to set priorities. Whenever you're struck with fear that you will not be successful if you have a balanced

● **answers on the fly** When someone asks a question, the Worker Bee researches the answer, spends hours finding supporting evidence of her claims, and presents her findings three days later in a bound format. Focus instead on giving top-level answers to questions based on your own experience and knowledge. You'll find that they are usually as accurate as the researched answers, people will be thrilled they don't have to wait, and you'll have a lot less work to do in the long run.

mindset, remember that balance works for your role model. Remind yourself that you will actually do better if you ditch your Worker Bee ways.

4. Say "To Hell with the Cell"

Electronic devices have enabled the Worker Bee to take her projects everywhere. Though a cell phone is outstanding if you're using it to coordinate cocktail hour with friends, it should not be ringing with work-related tasks during your vacation or over the weekend. Not only is it annoying to you; just think about how annoying it is to everyone else on the beach or in the restaurant.

Make it known to your coworkers that you shut off all electronic devices when you're away, and don't even sneak a peek at your BlackBerry. If necessary, take a few hours during the workday to let your phone go to voice mail. Close out of e-mail and spend the time working instead of responding to people. Just because you can talk to someone electronically when you're at the gym or in the shower doesn't mean you have to.

> ## The time to relax is when you don't have time for it.
>
> Sydney J. Harris

5. Take a Day to Get Away

If you carry over vacation time every year, kick yourself and put an end to it. Always take every day you have coming to you, and call in sick once in a while too. Talk to older people in your office and they'll tell you that if they could do it over again, they would have called in sick more frequently in their youth. Once again, use the little white lie if you need to. No sane boss will bother to investigate your trip to the gynecologist or your great-aunt's funeral.

● **water cooler wisdom** A Worker Bee often tries to do everything on her own. Get to know your coworkers. Say "hello" in the hallway and network at business functions. If they know you well, they'll help you when you need it. You'll also learn more about the jobs they do, which also will work in your favor. The more you understand about the needs and challenges of the business you work for, the better equipped you'll be to contribute to its success.

6. Toss a Crappy Boss

Sometimes a boss is a Worker Bee, and there's absolutely nothing you can do to change that. If you have a workaholic boss, she will not understand your need to live a balanced life. Ditch her immediately, even if it means leaving your job for a better one or changing departments. Working for people who respect your personal life and have a life of their own is crucial to being happy on a daily basis. Don't expect to change the culture or people you're working with. Instead, be proactive about finding a situation that works for you and allows you to stay sane.

7. Don't Feel Bad for Getting Mad

A Worker Bee sometimes feels guilty for asserting herself. Whether she's stating that a task is unnecessary, asking an underling to do something, or speaking up with her ideas in a meeting, she views herself as being bitchy or angry. Never feel

Every oak tree started out as a couple of nuts who stood their ground.

Anonymous

bad for being assertive, speaking your mind, and putting your foot down if someone is dumping work on you. What you think is anger, others see as a good, solid display of self-esteem. So don't feel guilty or kick yourself if you open your mouth. Instead, celebrate your spunky side. Being a team player does not mean being a doormat.

8. Know the Power of One Hour

You don't have to go across the globe to feel like you've taken a vacation. Leave it all behind on the weekend by driving just one hour from where you live. That's all it takes to gain perspective and feel relieved of the daily grind.

On the other hand, an hour is a powerful tool during the work week as well. Don't return phone calls for at least an hour after you receive them. Most of the time, the person asking for something will solve her own problem if you don't respond right away. You'll also train people to call you in advance for things they need. The power of an hour can create distance between you and a stressful situation, so use it to your advantage.

9. Be Bold and Ask for the Gold

A Worker Bee often spends endless hours toiling away but doesn't feel adequately compensated for her work. Remember that your job is a partnership with your employer—you work for the company, and it owes you compensation for what you do. Don't wait for someone to notice that you are worthy; speak up and ask for a raise or promotion. Be confident in what you do

● standup comic If you have trouble asking your boss something, try making a joke out of it first: "I'm getting a 200 percent raise, right? No, seriously, do you know what I can expect this year?" Sometimes making a little joke eases everyone into the conversation and sets the stage for more open communication.

and make sure others know how you're contributing to the success of the company. If you find yourself putting in long hours regularly, at the very least make sure that you're being paid adequately for your trouble. The squeaky wheel gets the grease, so squeak away.

10. Put "You" Before What You Do

The word "selfish" has a bad rap, but being selfish can be a really good thing for a Worker Bee. She, more than anyone, needs to put her own needs first.

If you are exhausted and want to take a day off, do it. If you need a cup of coffee, go outside and get it. If you have too much to do and you are losing your mind, tell your boss you need some relief. When you feel rested, well compensated, and fulfilled, you will actually have more energy to give and you'll perform better in everything you do. So do yourself a favor and be a little bit selfish sometimes.

When you make these ten workplace tips a part of your daily life, they will help you put distance between yourself and your work even when you're sitting in the office with a phone ringing in your ear. You'll be able to relax more often and you'll feel that you have the right to speak up, set priorities, and leave at a decent hour. But you still might have to remind yourself regularly that you deserve a break. So keep these ten tips pinned up nearby, and remember how important it is to find that middle ground between beach bum and bonkers: balance!

● the secret to silence Even if you sit in a cubicle, you too can have quiet time at work. Purchase a small pair of earplugs and use them for a few hours each day. They block out the chatter and the sniffles of officemates, giving you the time you need to focus on the tasks at hand.

● one day i'll . . . . If you have a habit of putting things off until you have your life under control, realize now that this magical moment when all your work is done will never come. Enjoy your life today and make time for yourself amidst the chaos.

Buzzing on to Better Days

The Worker Bee phase is that time in a woman's life when she puts her nose to the grindstone for a while. She works, cleans, listens, contributes, goes to graduate school—twice—and still has time to do her nails. She is Superwoman. But she can't remain a workaholic stress-head forever. So eventually she comes up for air and finds a more balanced way to live her life. She takes the steps necessary to reclaim her personal space, separate herself from her work, and celebrate life outside the office. She remains responsible but ditches work on occasion for family, friends, and fun. This lesson of balance is one that stays with her as she leaves her Worker Bee phase behind her for good.

It's true hard work never killed anybody, but I figure, why take the chance?

Ronald Reagan

Real Life Tales from Worker Bees

❝I cried because I didn't get invited to a meeting. I thought it meant I wasn't important. Now I am thankful when I don't get invited.❞

❝I gave my boss my home phone number to use over the weekend. It was only my second day on the job.❞

66 I made my way into the office through a blizzard. It took me three hours to get there and when I arrived, everyone else was still home. 99

66 I used to waste at least fifteen minutes of my day making labels on a label maker for all my folders. Now I jot the names in black marker and no one has noticed the difference. 99

66 I had food poisoning and I went to work anyway. I had to leave an hour after I got there and I puked all the way home. 99

66 I stayed up all night working on a report and the next day my boss was actually angry because I spent so much time on it. 99

66 A senior executive took my coffee cup out of the kitchen thinking it was his and I was afraid to speak up because I thought I would offend him. If that happened today, I would grab the thing out of his hand mid-sip. 99

theparty**girl**
like, call me on my cell

the party girl at a glance

nickname
Cocktail Queen, Darling (pronounced Dahhhling)

look
Ready to air-kiss at a moment's notice.

fashion
Anything slinky, sexy, and "oh so in."

phrase
"It is so wonderful to see you. You look absolutely fabulous."

love interest
At least ten different guys who are fun and ready to party at the drop of a hat.

favorite songs
Club mixes and fun, hip tunes.

events/activities
Dinners, bars, and parties, even on a work night.

friends
Everyone cool who likes to go out; a large clique of highly social female friends.

life goal
Life goal? There's plenty of time to figure that out.

Her cell phone rings like crazy and she drinks wine with a straw. She has 300 numbers stored in her BlackBerry, and those are just new additions from the last two weeks. She knows every formula for dealing with a hangover, how to look alert at work on three hours of sleep, and how to identify funky shoes that hurt less after three martinis. She is the primetime Party Girl.

Most women go through a phase when they just can't get enough of the nightlife, the day life, and everything in between—clubs, bars, dinners, movies, group trips, networking luncheons, and even regular chats with the Starbucks cashier. With a salary to spend on drinks and an appetite for meeting lots of new people, there's no stopping the Party Girl once she steps out onto the scene.

Nothing makes you more tolerant of a neighbor's noisy party than being there.

Franklin P. Jones

● attention-getting gear   Want to make people sit up and take notice of your group of friends in a bar? Try wearing something that makes people look your way, like a candy necklace or a cowboy hat. Nothing makes cute guys want to speak to a group of girls like these funny party props.

The Party Girl phase is a necessary time in every girl's life—it's as frivolous as it is fun. It's the time for every girl to sow her wild oats, show off her sexiest outfits, and dance until dawn. If she does it right and has the time of her life, she'll learn crucial lessons in social graces and make friends she'll never forget. She'll leave this phase behind but have memories for years to come of the time when life was wild, crazy, and absolutely fabulous.

Are You a Party Girl?

Life as a popular party girl is a wacky and wonderful time full of drinks, glitter, and guys galore. Though you might have gone through a party period as a teenager, sneaking beers when your parents are out of town is nothing compared to the glitz and glam of life as a social queen in the postcollege years. A Party Girl has no one around to stop her from going out, staying out until dawn on a work night, and blowing cash on drinks from the most extravagant martini menu in town. She is in control of her life and she can choose to do whatever she wants, whenever she wants—even if that means getting a little out of control now and then.

How do you know if you're in this phase? Review the following criteria and find out if you're a Party Princess or a Happy Homebody.

Full-Blown Party Princess

A Party Princess pours herself a drink, and then another (and yet another?) all before she gathers her girl group and heads out the door. Thursday through Sunday and sometimes Monday through Wednesday too, she's out on the scene as much as possible. You'll know you're a full-blown Party Princess if you:

❋ Love loud music and thumping club songs enough to play them in your car on a Sunday afternoon.

❋ Know more people than the mayor of your town does, and run into them everywhere—in the post office, the grocery store, and your living room at 4 A.M.

❋ Have mastered a face you like to call "the martini smile."

❋ Have more drink charges than anything else on your monthly credit card bill.

❋ Update your "going out" wardrobe more often than your work wardrobe.

❋ Often do the "walk of shame," i.e., spend the night at a guy's place and make your way home the next day wearing your wrinkled-up dress from the night before.

❋ Can speed-read subtitles, a skill learned from watching too much bar TV.

❋ Never leave home without your bottle opener.

❋ Know the bouncers at the local establishments by name.

❋ Think five hours in bed is a great night's sleep.

❋ Can recognize the guy you met even after the lights in the club come on.

❋ Know which bars in town have the best after-work cocktails, which have the hottest men, and which have bartenders who give you free drinks.

❋ Can handle any bathroom—squat, kneel, balance on one foot, sit—as long as it has a toilet.

❋ Are always game for going out, even when a hurricane is looming or it's forty below.

Know Your Buzz

The Early Buzz: Occurring at the start of the evening after a drink or two, the early buzz causes a Party Girl to feel happy and light—she has the whole evening ahead of her to have fun.

The Late Buzz: The type of buzz that occurs after you've lost count of your drinks and the room begins to spin. Often results in sitting on a curb yelling "I love you" to people you don't know.

Happy Homebody

A Happy Homebody is either a pooped-out Party Princess or a diva in dire need of a couple of margaritas and a friend to drag her out the door. You'll know you're a Happy Homebody if you:

* Go to the movies once a week and it makes you exhausted.
* RSVP for parties and never show up.
* Get all of your hip lingo and knowledge of other people from TV or a chat room.
* Have a cocktail and can't get out of bed for three days.
* Suggest a cool, hip bar only to discover it's been closed for two years.
* Use "I don't feel well" more than once a month to get out of going out after work.
* Only receive two phone calls a week on your $100 cell phone, and one of them is from your mother.
* Think a good party involves five-year-olds and a clown.

If being a Happy Homebody is your style, enjoy every minute of it. Just don't forget to live it up once in a while on the party scene. A good night of drinks and dancing will at the very least give you a new appreciation of the quieter life you love, and of course, you'll have fun too.

My grandmother is over eighty and still doesn't need glasses. Drinks right out of the bottle.

Henny Youngman

Diva Dictionary

A true Party Girl speaks a fun language she learned exclusively through her nights out on the scene. She uses old terms in new ways to communicate pertinent social issues to like-minded diva friends. If you find yourself nodding as you read the following terms, you are already fluent in Party Girl lingo.

Dating Guise: The nose and mustache you wear to escape talking to weirdos. After "dating guys" you don't like, you run right out and purchase a "dating guise."

Dave: The name of every guy you gave your phone number to on the Friday night when you weren't catching last names.

Greasy Diner Eggs: The not-so-wholesome breakfast food that tastes fabulous at 4 A.M. but makes your stomach churn the next morning.

Going-Out Friend: That girl you hang out with exclusively on weekends when you're going to a bar or party. Snow, sleet, hail, monsoon, she's on the phone urging you gently, and sometimes not so gently, to get your butt out the door and join her for a drink.

High Fashion: The four-inch heels that seem like a good idea at the beginning of the evening.

Martini Moment: Any time during the night that is so embarrassing, humiliating, or bizarre that you wish you had another martini to make it go away.

Men's Room: A convenient alternative to waiting in line for an hour. First turn the "M" upside down. Then leave your eyes open just enough to make a stealth entry, find your way to a stall, and make a swift exit.

Monkey Bars: Once a metal structure you swung across in the park, this phrase now refers to the dingy hangouts frequented by men with less than human brain power.

Moobs: Man boobs. Stay away from guys in the bar who are younger than 45 but have visible moobs.

Potty Pal: The buddy you met in line while waiting to use the bathroom. She knows your life story; she's seen you fix your bra; and, she was kind enough to hold the stall door shut for you.

Pregame Stash: The alcohol you keep on hand to drink before you go out. Has absolutely nothing to do with an athletic event.

The Truth: The answer you give after a few cocktails when a friend asks, "Do I look fat in this outfit?"

To-Go Cup: The plastic cup filled with a refreshing cocktail that you take with you when you leave the bar or party. You only fill it halfway and hide it carefully inside your coat.

If you speak this special language, you are a prime-time Party Girl. You know what drinks to order, what dress to wear, and how to tell your friend she's too good for the guy she's talking to without him catching on. You are the queen of the social scene.

Superb Social Training

Okay, so the Party Girl phase might be a little frivolous. But a girl's stint as a party princess is not without purpose. It is one of the

● **test your bartender** Find out how cool the bartender is at any establishment. Ask him to make you an obscure drink like a "Screaming Orgasm." A good bartender will give it a go even if he thinks you're nuts for asking for it.

most valuable phases she'll go through, teaching her lessons about life she can't learn any other way, like how to walk down a flight of stairs gracefully while holding a cocktail and how to apply lipstick without a mirror in a dark, crowded bar. So unless you are dreaming about living alone on an island or hiding out as a hermit, read on and learn why you should take your turn as a Party Girl.

A Party Girl Can Handle Unique Social Predicaments

Spending so much time interacting with others in close quarters allows you to master the social graces you need to survive as a Party Girl. You might fall face-first onto the sidewalk after that buzz-induced dizzy spell, but if you're a Party Girl, you pick yourself up, brush yourself off, and walk back into the club gracefully. You're a pro at handling yourself under the influence of alcohol,

When a Bar Is Sub-par

You can tell pretty quickly if the establishment you're in is not worth your time. Look for these signs that a bar is sub-par.

- The bartender waters down your drinks to the point that they are one step away from Evian.
- Regardless of what corner you move to, you end up sandwiched between two sweaty people.
- The bar charges a cover even though only three people are inside.
- You are reluctant to tip the bartender because the drink prices are so outrageous.
- The place is full of kids who look young enough to be in middle school.
- You buy ten rounds of drinks and the bartender doesn't offer you a freebie.
- Regulars entertain on the karaoke machine in lieu of real music.
- Only one bathroom stall awaits patrons, and it is dirty, mucky, and the door doesn't shut.

• never be the drunk-dialing drama queen. The drunk dialer has a few cocktails and then decides it is the perfect time to catch up with friends, family, ex-boyfriends, coworkers, and even her boss. If your finger gets the itch to dial away after you've had a few drinks, try to do something more productive with your hands, like clapping them to the beat of a funky dance tune.

loud music, and too few hours of sleep. You know to wipe your lipstick off with a napkin before sipping your drink. You've learned to speak slowly and loudly so your sober friends can understand what you're saying. You even know enough to check the bottom of your shoes for toilet paper after your trip to the ladies' room.

A Party Girl Goes After What She Wants

If you're a true Party Girl, you also know how to get your way in any party situation. When the random guy tries to grab you, you swat at him and yell out an obscenity to put him in his place. When the bartender isn't serving you fast enough, you know how to get his attention and get him moving. You know just what you want and how to get it because you've spent so many nights competing against the masses in poorly lit, overcrowded clubs.

A Party Girl Gets Creative

As a Party Girl, you know that waiting in line is just wasting precious minutes you could be spending in the club. So early on in the game you identify creative ways to get ahead. You're courageous and shrewd, playing to win and making it to the front of any queue in record time. Here are some quick Party Girl tips for getting to the front—fast.

The Exclusive Club Line

No guy with a clipboard will stop you. When trying to infiltrate the line at the newest club—so new it doesn't even have a name yet—a Party Girl has got to have her lines down and her costume carefully coordinated. So assemble your entourage, put on your best expressionless "I'm a celeb" face, and work your magic.

The Bathroom Line

The line for the bathroom is the most unforgiving of any line a Party Girl encounters in her quest for the ultimate night-life, so you know that to get ahead you have to play a little dirty. In extreme circumstances, try "crying menstrual" if necessary to get ahead. Or opt to hold your stomach and charge the stall like you have no more than seconds before you spew.

The Bar Line

A savvy Party Girl can get herself to the front of the bar in no time! The "Excuse me, I'm with that guy up there at the front" line can come out of your mouth more than a dozen times. If all else fails, make friends with whomever is right up against the bar playing with the napkins and you'll have your drink quicker than you can say "appletini."

The Cab Line

Who can stop you from getting in a cab first when you tell them you just received an emergency cell-phone call that your sister is having her baby? Cut that line and grab your cab.

The Coat Check Line

Coat check line? What coat check line? You have a secret place in the club to stick your belongings. As a regular, you deserve perks and privileges.

● drink-o-meter Remember, guys don't always mean what they say or say what they mean, especially when under the influence of alcohol. If he says, "Can I buy you a drink?" check the status of his glass. If it's full, he's interested in you. If it's empty, he might just be a drunk looking for another excuse to belly up to the bar.

Social Translator

Still struggling to interpret social lingo? This handy little device translates the true meaning of words and phrases said on the social scene:

Social Saying: Excuse me!
Translation: Please move.

Social Saying: You look great.
Translation: I can tell you want me to notice how you look so I will humor you.

Social Saying: I'm so happy for you.
Translation: You wench. You definitely did not deserve that raise.

Social Saying: It's so nice to see you.
Translation: I tried to dodge you when I saw you walk in the room but we made eye contact and so I had to say "hi."

Social Saying: Can I buy you a drink?
Translation: I want a drink myself but know it would be rude to desert you and head for the bar.

Social Saying: Really?
Translation: You never shut up, so I'm trying to say as little as I can in return to see if you'll fizzle out.

Social Saying: It's so loud in here.
Translation: I'm far too tired to make any effort to talk to you right now, so I'm using the first excuse I can come up with to get out of the conversation.

Social Saying: Your makeup looks different.
Translation: What happened to your face? Did your three-year-old niece go crazy with a box of markers?

Social Saying: So funny!
Translation: If you were actually comical at all, I'd be laughing, not saying "so funny."

Reminds me of my safari in Africa. Somebody forgot the corkscrew and for several days we had to live on nothing but food and water.

W. C. Fields

A Party Girl Knows How to Read Subtle Signs

As a Party Girl, you learn to understand the subtle nuances of human behavior because you interact with so many different people every night. You know how to identify the "help me" facial expression your friend makes when she's talking to a horrible guy. You recognize the creep disguised as a stud and you can see through your best buddy's "I'm sober enough to drive" façade. You are streetwise and barwise. You trust your instincts, and this edge helps you protect yourself in precarious situations.

A Party Girl Is Versatile

Countless nights out have honed your Party Girl instincts and given you the ability to look and feel great in any situation, without the creature comforts of home. From wardrobe challenges to bathroom adventures, you handle everything with grace, style, and attitude. Thanks to living life as a Party Girl, you can:

* ❋ Skillfully put on makeup in a dim bathroom with an inadequate mirror while waiting for a toilet stall to open up.
* ❋ Walk forty blocks in four-inch heels while never once losing your Party Girl strut.
* ❋ Survive outside with no coat in the dead of winter.

● **martini musts** Always leave a half an inch on top of your martini to avoid spillage, or ask for it in a giant beer mug.

✳ Hail a cab with one hand while eating gooey pizza with the other.

✳ Remember who gave you the phone number etched on the napkin in your handbag.

✳ Carry powder, lipstick, money, a tampon, a bank card, and your driver's license all on the side of your bra.

✳ Carefully disguise your emergency toilet paper stash on the other side.

✳ Talk bouncers into letting you in the door for free.

✳ Locate the ideal place to get cell phone reception in any club.

✳ Nurse a hangover with a fruity alcoholic morning drink.

These lessons in the art of being a social starlet stay with the Party Girl for a lifetime, bringing a smile to her face long after her days on the scene are over. So live it up and have the time of your life during this phase. Then you'll move on to calmer, quieter days with no regrets.

Sizing Up Strangers

The Party Girl can handle herself out on the social scene, but she has to deal with other people too. She meets cute men, cool chicks, and creepy strangers. She has to determine quickly when to talk and when to walk. So she develops a strategy for sizing up the scene around her.

Start with the Obvious

Always start with the most obvious clues. By paying attention to someone's look, dress, and demeanor you can get a general idea of what type of person you're dealing with. Does he leave his shirt undone one button too far? Is she wearing a skirt that gives you full view of her thong underwear? You can assume

● tattoo travesty Be open to trying new activities but just say no to the tarantula tattoo that a friend suggests after a few cocktails.

that these people have "revealing" personalities and avoid them if that kind of thing isn't for you. Likewise, if a guy looks like he bought out the fluorescent orange jacket collection at Wal*Mart or he's wearing a camouflage suit but never spent a day in his life in the armed forces, you can assume he might enjoy hunting in his spare time. Through simple observation, you can glean important information about the people around you and make smart choices about how to spend your party time.

Pay Attention to What He's Drinking

When you walk into a roomful of interesting people, check out each person's beverage. You can tell so much about a person by what he or she is drinking. Use this handy guide to help you along.

The Martini

This drink exudes classic sophistication and is favored by veteran Party Girls everywhere. Martini Guys are harder to come by. Be thankful if you're lucky enough to find one. If he's choosing a martini, it shows that he has discerning taste in drinks—which probably carries over into other areas of his life. But watch out—he might have ordered a martini because he's trying too hard to impress the ladies!

Extra tip: You can assume that anyone holding a martini has good coordination. It takes a very steady hand to avoid spillage with one of these babies.

Adventure is worthwhile in itself.
Amelia Earhart

Wine

Wine is a tricky elixir. A true Party Girl drinks wine only when there's a stellar wine list to choose from. You'll know she knows her stuff if she sticks with a refreshing Sauvignon Blanc or a classic Cabernet.

If you spot a guy with a glass of wine, he could be Metro or Euro, making him a great candidate for interesting conversation. A nice glass of wine says "Details are important to me."

Extra tip: Steer clear of the guy drinking white zinfandel. Unlike other wines, a glass of white zin usually says "I live at home with my mother and don't have a job."

Beer

While a Party Girl has a beer now and then, beer has one real purpose: to tell all about the types of guys in the crowd. One rule applies here: type of beer = type of guy. The guys don't have to speak—their beer speaks for them. Check out this handy beer translator:

Coors Light: "I just graduated from college and I miss my frat brothers."

Budweiser: "I'm really into monster truck rallies."

Colt 45 wrapped in a paper bag: "I hardly have enough money to buy new underwear, let alone this beer."

Hard cider: Hard cider of any kind is just a mistake.

Harvey Wallbanger

A fashionable drink from the 1970s, this cocktail says one of two things about the guy who orders it: he has spent one too many nights with his parents, or he's reading a book on the retro scene. Determine his reasons for choosing this refreshing cocktail before giving him your number.

Fuzzy Navel

A true newcomer to social situations orders a Fuzzy Navel. This drink says "I attend wedding receptions regularly." The drinker is uncorrupted by the trendy social scene. Take him by the hand and show him the way to a fun-filled evening.

Rum and Diet Coke

Any Diet Coke mixer lets you know that person is watching his weight. If he's already thin, he might be a little bit anal retentive, so avoid him. If he's chubby, on the other hand, give him some credit for trying to shed the pounds.

Margarita

The ultimate frou-frou drink. A girl drinking margaritas can be the newest addition to your Party Girl entourage. Get to know her and soon you'll be dancing on the bar and bonding.

If a guy looks comfortable drinking margaritas, he probably has female friends who influence him, a very good thing indeed. Of course, he also may be gay, especially if the drink is pink.

Extra tip: Throw all of the previous rules out the window if a beach is nearby. Then any icy concoction goes.

Jack Daniels

A true "manly man" drink. If a guy is drinking Jack Daniels, he's a fun partier but he might not be that stable to date at this time in his life. He's the one who will end up face down in the gutter hours after the bar closes.

Flaming Sambuca

A trademark drink of Euro hotties! If you want to practice your French, meet the person behind this fiery shot.

Hear Every Word

Don't let a guy's cute face or the magic of the moment overtake you so much that you ignore the words coming from his mouth. Is he a Whitesnake fan who just can't let go? Are three of his ex-girlfriends missing? If he tells you something that doesn't sit right, don't laugh it off. Run like hell. If you hear any of the following comments during a conversation, take your drink and flee quickly:

* ✳ "Oh, I went there three years ago, when I last saw my kids."
* ✳ "My wife told me to get home early."
* ✳ "Those damn cops keep showing up at my house."
* ✳ "My attorney suggested an insanity defense."
* ✳ "I can't get rid of this itchy rash I picked up in South America."
* ✳ "She wouldn't shut up so I shut her up."
* ✳ "I always wondered what it would be like to be a woman."
* ✳ "Where's your friend with the cute ass?"
* ✳ "I can't tell you what I do for a living. It's a secret."
* ✳ "Park benches can be really comfortable."
* ✳ "Quick! Hide! There's that girl I borrowed money from."

My mother used to say that there are no strangers, only friends you haven't met yet. She's now in a maximum security twilight home in Australia.

Dame Edna Everage

Live It Up!

A best friend can turn into a nuisance faster than you can swallow a Jell-O shot, and a cute guy prospect can turn into a total nightmare after his second beer, but that doesn't mean you should avoid people altogether for fear these things will happen. Be cautious enough to avoid freaks and geeks, but don't go overboard and become so paranoid that you hide in a corner all night. Deal with annoying people tactfully so you can reach the ultimate goal—having fun. Never squander an opportunity to make cool friends, meet great guys, and live it up Party Girl style.

Watch What He Does

Finally, find out more about a guy by observing his actions. A caring person shows consideration through the little things, like offering you a napkin if you spill your drink on your hand or getting up so you can sit down after a long night of dancing. Try to separate drunk moves from things he would also do if he were sober. If he trips, bumps into you, and doesn't say "I'm sorry" because he doesn't feel a thing, that's a drunk move. On the other hand, if he takes your number and then takes your friend's number as well, he's questionable.

Never give a party if you will be the most interesting person there.

Mickey Friedman

Take a Breather

Even the most energetic party chick can use a glass of ice water and a nap on occasion. When you're feeling the urge to relax and hide out from the world, take a day or two for yourself, rest, and then re-enter the social scene in style.

Stop Signs

You might realize you need a break when you wake up feeling as if every bone in your body is broken. Pay attention to signs that you are in dire need of a breather and heed them. They include things like these:

* Your family complains that they only get to talk to you when you call them drunk at 3 A.M. on your cell.
* Every article of clothing you own is sleek, sexy, and smells like smoke.
* You've gone through an entire bottle of pain reliever tablets in a month.
* A special rubber band sits next to the toilet for when you need to tie your hair back and hurl.
* You spend more money on drinks than you do on food.
* You request a club song at the church picnic.
* You choose your work outfit every day based on whether or not you can also wear it out at night.
* You get phone calls regularly from guys you don't know who claim you gave them your number.
* Your eyes hurt when the lights are too bright because you're used to spending time in dimly lit venues.
* Your friends nickname you "The Lush."

If these signs ring true, turn off your phone, draw a warm bath, and take a breather for a while. Even though going out is fun, it can be a lot of work. If you keep doing it over and over again without a break, you'll burn out. Take time to rejuvenate so you always look and feel your best when you're out there playing Party Girl.

The Five-Step Sanity Plan

Are you so caught up in the social scene that you have no idea how to relax? Is your idea of a breather taking a step outside the club for a smoke? No matter how much you love the night-life, follow this five-step rejuvenation plan on occasion to keep your life in order and your energy levels high.

Step 1: Clean Off the Bar Smell

When you get home at night from a party or bar, your clothes will reek of a unique combination of scents including beer, liquor, smoke, and that musty, too-many-people-in-a-room smell. Begin your R&R by gathering up all your bar gear and putting it in the wash. Then dump over your mini-purse, which you haven't cleaned in months, and get the stuff out of there that's starting to rot—the fuzz balls, the matchbooks, and the pieces of napkin. If your going-out clothes sit there staring at you, you're going to feel the urge to wear them again or to go shopping for something new to wear out. So get these items out of your sight for a few days so you can rest.

Step 2: Resist the Urge to Talk to Your Going-Out Friends

Your going-out friend is the friend who can convince you to get out of your pajamas and into a miniskirt at midnight

You can discover more about a person in an hour of play than in a year of conversation.

Plato

Not to mention, who really wants to talk to the same person for an entire year.

Party Girl

• looks can kill Never don the "everyone's looking because I'm so beautiful" face.

on a Tuesday. When you're out with her, she says, "Come on . . . come on . . . stay out an hour longer." She is always egging you on to stay for one more drink and one more song. When you're taking a breather, turn off the phone and hide from this friend. Crawl under the bed if you need to. If she gets ahold of you, she'll convince you that you're missing something stupendous by staying in for a night and you'll fall for it. Soon that sneaky girl will have you out the door in heels and a boa. Darn her!

Step 3: Say Goodbye to Vampire Hours

You might not feel tired at 10 P.M. because you're so used to being up late. In fact, you're thinking, "It's before midnight! The evening has just begun!" Once in a while, try to get back on a regular sleeping schedule. Wake yourself up bright and early and go for a jog (yeah, right) or more realistically, roll out of bed before 11 A.M. and pat yourself on the back for starting your day before noon. Say goodbye to vampire hours and get your body clock back on real-world time for a few days. You'll feel more rested once you do.

Step 4: Drink Fluids (Cocktails Don't Count!)

The Party Girl experiences dehydration on a regular basis from alternating evenings drinking alcohol with mornings drinking extra-large cups of coffee. If you're getting headaches and feeling fatigued, you might be dehydrated and not even realize it. So take an ice-water break and cleanse the alcohol out of your system. Carry a bottle of water with you and sip it regularly. You can also use it to splash your going-out friend if she won't leave you alone.

Step 5: Be Lame for a Night

Once you're well rested and hydrated, spend at least one low-key night at home watching movies or reading. Catch up on all of those important things you need to do that you've let fall by the wayside, like eating, calling your mother, and cleaning your apartment. If you're a true Party Girl, after one night in you'll be energized and ready to get back out on the scene again.

Get It While You Can

The Party Girl has dinner with dancers, martinis with mad-men, and she bellies up to the bar with brilliant babes. She knows thousands of people, has a knack for making friends wherever she goes, and also has an unquenchable thirst for cocktails that no number of Long Island iced teas can quench. This phase is fun, fabulous, and full of great times that keep a girl laughing long after these hectic days are over. So remember your Party Girl phase fondly and celebrate it. It's a once-in-a-lifetime bash.

Real-Life Tales from Party Girls

66 I brought a feather boa out to the bar. I danced around with it and every guy in the place wanted to talk to me. It's amazing that it only took a few pink feathers to break the ice. 99

66 I drank too much fruit punch and vodka, forgetting there is a lag between when you drink it and when it hits you. I spent the night hurling in the bathroom and my friends have photos of me leaning over the toilet. 99

66 We would always end up eating in places at 4 A.M. that we would never dream of going to sober. McDonald's, Taco Bell, White Castle, you name it. We showed no discretion. 99

❝ It would be below zero out but we wouldn't want to have to worry about checking our coats, so we would leave them in the car and walk outside for blocks to get to a bar. ❞

❝ I went on so many first dates one summer with guys I met out that I felt like I was interviewing people for a position. ❞

❝ I rode a mechanical bull in my bra at a rodeo bar because I wanted to be the life of the party. My friends insist that bar uses the pictures of me from that night in their advertisements. ❞

chapter 5

thebody-
consciousbabe
vitamins and mineral water

the body-conscious babe at a glance

nickname
Workout Girl, Fitness Freak, Nutrition Queen

look
Energized, sporty, and ready to run a 5K.

fashion
Sneakers, shorts, a sports bra, and a bottle of water.

phrase
"I'll have the fat-free, low-carb, sugar-free brownie [that tastes like straw], and a Diet Coke."

love interest
"Active guy," the one who plays sports and loves to go to the gym.

favorite songs
"I Want Candy" by Bow Wow Wow and sometimes, "Running on Empty" by Jackson Browne.

events/activities
Yoga class, long jogs through the park, and Runners Club meetings.

friends
Her exercise buddy, her Pilates instructor, and the cashier at the New Balance store.

life goal
To run the New York, Boston, and London marathons in under three hours (okay, under four).

A time comes in every girl's life when she stops living on Pepsi and potato chips, resolves to get in shape, and starts working out like a maniac. She wakes up one day, stares at her pink processed Pop-Tart and thinks, "I might get rickets if I don't start eating real food." So she commits to changing her body and her life for the better in one grand sweep.

During this phase, a girl wears the soles of her running shoes thin, keeps the vitamin companies in business, and considers topping even her pizza with sprouts. She's committed to getting in shape and staying in shape even if it means waking up at 6 on a Saturday morning to run. She makes time to go to the gym every day, keeps motivational notes pinned up on her bulletin board, and reads all she can about good nutrition. She is the Body-Conscious Babe (BC Babe).

Like all other phases in a woman's life, the BC Babe phase does eventually come to an end—no girl can resist junk food forever. But until she realizes that a little sugar is a good thing, she cuts cookies, carbs, and calories, feels guilty if she cheats on her diet, and takes healthful living to a new extreme.

Life as a BC Babe

Even if you're not a BC Babe now, you probably know someone who is. She works out religiously, reads fitness magazines on the train, and can recite the details behind all the studies that support the latest diet craze. Sometimes you wish you could emulate her health-conscious lifestyle.

Or maybe the BC Babe phase has already happened to you. You were going along each day, living your life and eating the way you always had and then BOOM, someone or something happened that pushed you over the edge and into extreme fitness. You decided you were going to look perfect and you resolved to change fifty things about your life to get there—all at once. From your hair to your diet, you read about the secrets of celebrities, tried new fads, and became a regular at the gym. For weeks or months you lived your life as a BC Babe.

Hallmarks of a Health Nut

BC Babes take many shapes and forms, but they all have one thing in common: they strive to be healthy day in and day out. How would you know a BC Babe is in your midst? She:

* ✳ Brings celery and carrots in a little plastic bag for lunch instead of brownies.
* ✳ Forgets to eat because she's so busy (does that really happen?).

● **but she's perfect?** Sometimes a BC Babe sees other women who appear thinner or more together and thinks, "She's perfect, so why can't I be?" The truth is that she's not, even if she appears that way at a glance, unless of course she's had lots of surgery. Every woman has flaws she can't stand and things about her body she wants to change, from weight to hair to skin to nails to everything. These feelings seem to be a natural part of everyone's life.

✳ Has a picture of an Olympic athlete or a swimsuit model that she aspires to be taped to her fridge

✳ Walks to work, takes the stairs, and uses a rowing machine while she watches television

✳ Orders fruit for dessert instead of peanut butter pie à la mode

✳ Receives chocolate as a gift and gives it all away to co-workers

✳ Swears that sugar-free ice cream tastes better than regular

✳ Knows the staff at the sports club well enough to invite them to her housewarming party

✳ Volunteers to lead the office volleyball team and running team

✳ Orders her coffee with skim

✳ Fits into all her "skinny" clothes

✳ Knows the difference between Sweet'N Low, Equal, and Splenda

✳ Orders salad at the all-you-can-eat restaurant

✳ Uses terms like Body Mass Index (BMI) and cardio

✳ Doesn't bring a T-shirt to cover up at the beach

✳ Tries to talk you into trying a new oranges and grapefruit diet

A BC Babe has little muscles in her arms and a spring in her step. She looks great, feels fabulous, and inspires even the most sluggish person to run a mile or two. She is a woman we admire and envy.

● up for debate Are nutrition bars good for you or simply a damn good excuse to have chocolate for breakfast? No one really knows. Until this debate is settled, go ahead and snack away on these vitamin-packed chocolate bars.

I burned sixty calories. That should take care of a peanut I had in 1962.

Rita Rudner

Different Kinds of BC Babes

From the runner and the vegetarian to the healthy mom and the mountain climber, BC Babes stay in shape in many different ways. But they all are gung-ho about what they do and they make it look easy to the rest of us.

The Athlete

She plays tennis after work and softball on weekends, and swims for relaxation. With her hair in a ponytail and random pieces of sports equipment in her gym bag, she's ready to play the game at a moment's notice.

The Vegetarian or Vegan

She makes the chef at the restaurant work for his money, ordering interesting entrées of her own creation and specifying "No egg! No fish!" When you order a steak, she gives you a laundry list of reasons why cutting out red meat will add years to your life.

The Mountain Climber

Not into traditional sports, she loves the great outdoors. She knows all the tricks for surviving at high altitudes and understands how to use oxygen to move up from base camp. Her vacations involve hikes on some of the world's most treacherous trails. She is truly a wonder to those of us who are less inclined to climb.

The Nutritionist

She knows what ratio of protein to carbs to fat will keep the human body in energy mode. She takes supplements, drinks vitamin infusion shakes, and sips herbal teas to build her immune system. If you want to know which foods to eat to make your hair stronger or your skin smoother, she has all the answers.

The Aerobics Babe

She works out to the latest techno beat with more rhythm than a professional dancer. She is never out of breath. She can count out loud with ease after forty-five minutes of jumping around to *Grease* tunes with weights in her hands. She's the only woman on the planet who looks fabulous in a skimpy, trendy exercise outfit.

The Runner

She belongs to a training group and her sole focus this year is qualifying for a marathon. Her legs are shapely, her body lean, and her feet able to endure pounding the pavement for miles. Others might huff and puff, but for her, working out is relaxing.

The Bodybuilder

She can bench-press more than the guy she's dating. People jokingly call her Schwarzenegger. Her arms and shoulders reveal muscles you never knew women had. When you ask her how she does it, she spouts out words like "sets" and "reps" that make you feel weak just thinking about them.

There is no sincerer love than the love of food.

George Bernard Shaw

The Jogger Mom

She bundles that kid up, plops him into an all-terrain stroller, and takes off for the park. You can see her running by, the baby sleeping while she works up a sweat. She's truly an inspiration, losing all her pregnancy weight in record time.

The Walk-aholic

She walks to work, the movies, and all of her appointments. She walks on her lunch hour, with her boyfriend, and with her best friend. She skips the elevator and walks to her tenth-floor apartment, carrying groceries.

Extreme Fitness

When you're a BC Babe, you look your best and feel great—a little tired from working out so often, but great nonetheless. You drop a size in jeans, get whistled at on the street, and have a strange, inexplicable power that allows you to resist the urge to order mozzarella sticks. A personal trainer's dream, you're motivated, energized, and ready to tackle the elliptical machine on maximum speed. You are the ultimate extreme fitness queen.

But the BC Babe wasn't always this motivated to look her best. Something occurred that pushed her over the edge and into the realm of extreme fitness. From the serious to the silly, certain forces in our lives prompt us to embark on the "I want to be perfect" kick. And once we do, we go all the way.

The Little Voices

Sometimes the little voices in your head push you to become the BC Babe. You feel that you're in a rut so you decide the easiest thing to do right off the bat is upgrade your fitness routine. You set out to perfect every muscle and star in your own exercise video. These little voices can creep into your head when you see a person jogging down the street, observe all the people in line for a salad at the deli, or hear a girl talk about how frequently she lifts weights. These voices remind you that you can always be doing something more to take care of your body. Sometimes you have the power to ignore them and grab a cookie anyway, but if they come at the wrong time, when you're feeling the need for a change in your life, they set you off on the road to extreme fitness.

You're egged on by the little voices that keep nagging you:

"You should do more to take care of yourself."

You haven't worked out in months. A feeling of guilt comes out of nowhere and overtakes you. You hear that little voice saying "You *should* work out more." "You *should* get up off the couch at night and go for a walk." "You *should* run twenty miles a day and lose twenty pounds." You would love to slap the little sucker whispering these messages in your ear, but instead you resolve to get your butt in gear and go to the gym every morning before work.

"Have vegetables instead."

After months of eating Häagen-Dazs for dinner five nights a week, the little voice says, "This is going to catch up with you if you don't stop." As you toss the last empty pint container into the garbage, you resolve to eat more vegetables and order the tall latte with skim instead of the grande with whole milk. You even clean out your cupboards, throw away the chips, and replace everything with new, healthful foods.

"One more mile, you wuss."

You are going to the gym faithfully but doing a halfhearted "walk-jog" routine. A lanky girl arrives at the same time you do and runs five miles at high speed. You decide you're going to push it from now on and put out all the effort you can. The little voice creeps in and says, "You can run one more mile you lazy kid. You're not tired yet." You decide to race that lanky chick and win . . . whether she knows it or not.

"If she can do it, so can you."

The coworker who used to be overweight is now teaching aerobics and looking fantastic. The little voice says, "If she can lose fifty pounds, you can lose five." So you find out what method she used to change her body and her life and you set out with all your willpower to do the same.

"You could fit into your favorite old jeans again."

A stack of clothes are piled high on the bed and though you look and feel great in most of them, that one pair of jeans from a few years ago stares back at you, mockingly. The little voice says, "Go ahead. Try to wiggle them on." You know they aren't going to fit but you aren't going to give up on them just yet. You hang them on the closet door for motivation and resolve to fit into them again even if it means eating celery for the next six months.

Important Occasions

Sometimes you become a BC Babe because a significant occasion is looming and you want to look like a superstar. You set your sights on your "goal weight" and become a fitness fanatic trying to reach it. Any important occasion can inspire a BC Babe to spend mornings at the gym, days counting calories, and nights trying on outfits to see her progress.

In the end, you hope to show up at your event looking great and feeling fabulous. When looking back at your BC Babe phase and all the time you spent working out, you'll probably be amazed you found the inspiration to do it!

Some of the more inspirational occasions include:

The Wedding

You go to the extreme to look good for a friend's wedding because you're sure you're going to see her cute cousin there. Or it's your own wedding and you are diehard about looking fabulous. After all, those photos are pricey and you want them to turn out well. You check the calendar, count how many months you have left to get in shape, and start working out like a maniac.

The High School Reunion

You're not going to let that annoying guy who always picked on you in high school do it again. You're going to show him, and everyone else, how great you look and feel. You experiment with a new hairstyle, try brighter makeup, softer makeup, no makeup, arched eyebrows, thicker eyebrows, and more, all in the name of looking good. Of course, on top of that, you start jogging and counting calories so you can fit into your favorite dress with ease.

The Business Function

You've been called upon to speak at the conference in six weeks and you don't want to look like a frumpy business lady. Not to mention, cute work guy will be there. You resolve to lose five pounds, get a tan, and wear your chic suit so you are an invincible powerhouse when you give your presentation.

The Big Date

Nothing can inspire a week-long stint as a BC Babe like a big date looming. He's the one you really like and you're going to look fabulous, be charming, and feel great when you see him for dinner next Saturday. You work out twice a day, eat salad for every meal, and read about new ways to do your makeup and hair. You even shop obsessively for the right thing to wear until you're so pooped out you can't set foot in another store.

The Tropical Vacation

If you're going to spend seven days on a cruise surrounded by all-you-can-eat buffets, cocktails, and bikini weather, you must prepare. You do stomach crunches, butt exercises, and get a little base tan so that when you show up, you can lounge on your deck chair without winning the "pasty chick" award. You even buy sunless tanner, try it out to make sure you don't turn orange, and then dip yourself in it headfirst.

PMS

PMS usually comes and goes and leaves a girl a little bit more bloated and weary for a week or two. But sometimes it takes on a new, more intensely evil form, wreaking havoc and destruction in her life. For whatever reason, some months it is as if hell built a house on earth and you're living in it. When this type of major PMS hits, it can drive any girl to have I-need-to-change-my-life thoughts that propel her into extreme fitness mode. She'll do anything to fight off her PMS pain or, at the very least, to recover from it when it's over. You'll know PMS is the cause of your newfound fitness fervor if you:

* Feel the urge to yell at the mailman for folding your magazines.
* Are certain, due to the size of your stomach, that you swallowed an entire watermelon at the family picnic.
* Find forty candy bar wrappers in your garbage can and can't remember where they came from.
* Have recently been nicknamed "Time Bomb" by your coworkers.
* Get teary-eyed when you're watching *Friends* reruns.
* Break down and cry when you can't find your pen.

So Many Products

How can a girl resist the urge to become a BC Babe when she's bombarded with so many new products, diets, and fitness crazes every day? You're bound to give one of them a try at some point in your life even if you don't consider yourself to be the fitness type at all.

A girl is often pushed into the BC Babe phase by momentum from her friends and the media. When enough people around you are on a diet kick, trying certain exercise machines or buying fat burners, you simply give in and give them a try. You develop your own extreme health routine and next thing you know, you're the one preaching the merits of the latest craze.

Diet Plans

Let's talk diet plans. Low carb! Low calorie! Low sugar! Low fat! Next it will be "Lose weight for life by eating paper towels." Your cousin lost ten pounds eating cabbage soup. Your mother dropped weight on Atkins. Your coworker is doing the South Beach diet and loving it. Can you resist the urge to try the new peanut butter diet just revealed in health journals everywhere? Chances are the answer is "no."

Devices

A new vibrating waist belt or foldup treadmill can tempt even the most discerning consumer. Who can really resist purchasing the Thighmaster when the pretty woman on TV insists it helped her lose fourteen pounds in two weeks? When new

● **extreme overhaul** Sometimes a girl feels the urge to redo her whole look during her time as a BC babe. Before you go for the lip implants or tummy tuck, sleep on your decision for a while and make sure it's not something you'll regret later. Don't let a temporary mood compel you to make an extreme decision with permanent consequences.

fitness products make it so easy to get exercise in your spare time, the BC Babe just has to give them a go.

Pills, Herbs, and Special Foods

The fat-burning herb, the appetite-suppressing tea, and the low-carb candy bars on the market can pique your interest even if you're as skinny as can be. They seem so wonderful, these automatic quick fixes. But do they work? Most people say "no," but it's still up for debate. That doesn't stop the BC Babe from giving them a try.

> No diet will remove all the fat from your body because the brain is entirely fat. Without a brain, you might look good, but all you could do is run for public office.
>
> George Bernard Shaw

Naysayers and Such

A BC Babe thinks three things: (1) I want to be in shape, (2) I want to stay in shape, and (3) I want people to notice my progress. So if someone says something contrary to a BC Babe's hopes for her future, she feels the urge to slap that person silly. The people the BC Babe wishes to avoid include:

* Doctors who say things like, "Your weight is very normal for your height and you're getting older. You can't expect to look good forever."
* Self-proclaimed fitness fanatics who say, "Oh, you need to try the kiwi diet. I know that's the one that will work for you."

❋ The boyfriend who says, "You lost weight? Oh, I thought you got a haircut or something."

❋ The aerobics instructor who says, "Tsk, tsk. You've missed three classes."

❋ Her mother, who says, "You always look the same to me."

❋ Her older sister, who insists, "You are still looking more and more like mom every day and there's nothing you can do about it even if you do work out."

These people drive her over the edge and make her work even harder toward her goals. They are the forces that light the fire under her. She feels even more of a need to achieve the perfect body because she wants to prove them wrong.

The cardiologist's diet: If it tastes good, spit it out.

Unknown

Back to Reality

The BC Babe phase may go on for weeks, months, or years. Or it may be over as quickly as it began. The end can be as simple as your mother calling one day and saying, "You really shouldn't cut out ice cream. You need the calcium." You think about her words for about, um, ten seconds and then go out, purchase a half-gallon of chocolate ice cream, and wolf it down. Your mother makes a good point. You can't deprive yourself forever. Your extreme fitness routine comes to a screeching halt and you're back to reality.

It is next to impossible to stay on a mega-health kick for a long time. These spurts of inspiration usually last at most a year,

● share praise freely Give compliments freely to all the women in your life. If we work together to build the self-esteem of those around us, we will put an end to the "I want to be perfect" phase for good.

but usually far less. It only takes a split second for something to shake you out of your fitness freak mode and into real life again, and there are plenty of people and situations around to do that.

Moments of Weakness

The evil forces of food and drink are everywhere. You can't escape them—and even if you try, they always find you. At business luncheons, birthday parties, and weekend getaways, you can bet that food will be the center of the occasion, bringing your time as a BC Babe to an end. Moments to watch out for include:

You're Visiting Mom

She's never going to let you pick at her homecooked meals. She's going to make sure you sample chocolate from all the candy dishes in the house. Don't even try to hide from this food-pushing lady.

There's Free Food at Work

From cookies in the kitchen to catered platters at the meeting, you're going to have to make a choice at some point: watch other people eat from afar or join in the fun.

It's a Big Night Out with Friends

You can show up late for the dinner at the Mexican restaurant hoping to miss out on the main part of the meal but you won't escape without having a few glasses of wine and finishing up the tortilla chips in the basket. If you're going to go that far, why not go all the way and order a cheese burrito and a fruity margarita?

the health hawk Avoid dating men who constantly comment on your weight or body. Your guy should only intervene in your six-month fudge sundae binge if you asked him to do so. A man who really loves you will not put you through army-style calisthenics or demand that you maintain supermodel style. If you feel that you have to earn his love, tell him to take a long, rigorous, healthy hike—without you.

It's the Holidays

Come on now, regardless of how much willpower you've mustered you will not resist party after party filled with sugar cookies, hors d'oeuvres, and eggnog. Only Scrooge says no to a rum ball.

Your Significant Other Orders Pizza

Your boyfriend brings over ice cream or orders a feast of Chinese food for delivery on a cold, rainy night. Are you really going to say no to the food and hop on the treadmill instead? You might as well join him and enjoy the sweet and sour chicken.

You're on Vacation

You're going out to dinner every night and eating fries and cotton candy on the boardwalk. Or your hotel package includes dinner with the price of your room. You have to get your money's worth, so you load up on the lobster.

You Have Guests in Town

You purchase several types of bagels plus cream cheese, eggs, bacon, and pancakes to make sure that your guests have enough to eat for breakfast at your place. Then you arrange to take them to a nice restaurant after you show them the town. Not only is it hard to eat just salad through all of this, but you have to explain why you're passing up the soft, buttered bread that comes with your meal. More likely than not, you're going to give in and eat with them.

You're Tired

If you feel utterly exhausted you're bound to turn to food for sustenance. A few pieces of chocolate with a grande cappuccino can pull you out of your zombie state of mind.

Everywhere you go, food stares back at you. You hear doughnuts whispering "eat me" in the middle of the night. You pass bakery windows filled with creamy delicacies and long to dig into a pastry puff. Before long you can't resist the power of food any longer. Your commitment to cutting out snacks, drinking lots of water, and saying no to bread gets tossed out the window. The longer you stick to your diet, the hungrier you get and the easier it is to give in. Eventually someone shows up at work with a box of chocolates and a bag of peanut butter cookies and you cave without shame.

The second day of a diet is always easier than the first. By the second day you're off it.

Jackie Gleason

The End Is Near

It is truly no fun at all to go through life skipping dessert and working out every day. In fact, it's downright painful to keep up this routine. So you cheat a little here, give in a little there. Then one day Satan himself invites you to a huge five-course Italian dinner and you give up on your BC Babe ways for good.

First, the hunger goes away. Then you are overcome with relief because your days of deprivation are over. You unhook the

The only miracle pill that will make everyone thin is the one that costs so much people don't have any money left over to buy food.

Anonymous

mileage counter from around your waist and cheer out loud as you toss it in the garbage. You realize that you can maintain your weight without being the Bionic Woman after all, and that's exactly what you plan to do. You know the end of your stint as a BC Babe has come when you:

❋ Stop the treadmill at 29:30 (round up!) and feel no guilt.

❋ Think other health nuts are a tad bit crazy.

❋ Ditch the idea for good that you'll actually lose weight by eating sandwiches from Subway.

❋ Decide your walk to work can replace your trip to the gym.

❋ Hear the phrase "Guys like girls with a little oomph" and it makes a lot of sense.

❋ Resign yourself to wearing one size larger.

❋ Admire your friends who eat everything and don't care.

❋ Put the scale in the closet or throw the damn thing out.

❋ Tackle your boyfriend when he tries to eat the chocolate your mother sent you.

❋ Rationalize that sleeping in will do more for your health than working out will.

You realize it's just physically and emotionally impossible to be that good for that long. So you bite into a brownie, enjoy every morsel of it, and say "to hell with this fitness stuff" once and for all.

Ditching the Diet

It can be a huge relief to give up on a strict diet and just let your body do what it does on its own without fighting it. Not to mention, it makes you a hell of a lot more fun to be around because you're not hungry all the time and you don't need special foods when you're out with friends. If you've ditched your diet recently, there are plenty of reasons to celebrate. Don't feel guilty, be happy.

Celebrate because . . .

✻ Well-fed people are always in a better mood than their dieting counterparts.

✻ You look healthy and have more energy when you don't feel famished.

✻ You won't bug your friends with the phrase, "There's nothing edible on this fondue menu."

✻ Regular foods are a heck of a lot cheaper than diet foods.

✻ Having a good junky snack at work makes the day a little brighter.

✻ You'll no longer get "I'm starving" headaches.

✻ You can say goodbye to the guilt you normally feel for ruining your diet.

Enjoy the freedom that comes from giving in to your body's natural needs. Celebrate both the end of your time as a BC Babe and all of the good things about normal eating.

Realizations

Is it even healthy to diet and work out like a maniac? Eventually the BC Babe comes to the realization that it isn't. As with everything else, moderation is the key. All that pressure on your joints from jogging is a little too much to bear. It is stressful to fit a workout into your schedule every day and constantly worry about what is going in your mouth. Something about living this way just doesn't feel right.

When your days as a BC Babe are over, you accept certain realities about your body and your life, most notably that you can't be perfect and neither can anyone else. It's not really worth it to invest so much time and energy into carrying out an extreme plan for fitness and nutrition when the goal of perfection is just not attainable. You accept that:

✳ You can't change the shape of your body completely. You just are what you are and working out can only enhance your natural shape.

✳ Losing weight doesn't solve all your problems. It can make you feel a little bit more confident but in the end, you have to believe in yourself and your worth regardless of how frequently you go to the gym.

✳ Diets suck. Diet foods are disgusting, inedible, and dry as hell. Food is a part of life and it's no fun to hide from it.

✳ Most diets don't work. Though some people achieve moderate success through diet plans, nothing ever works as well as the "everything in moderation" principle.

✳ There is an optimal level of fitness. You can go too far with your workout routine and absolutely destroy your joints. More is not always better when it comes to exercising.

✳ Guys like women for their confidence and energy, and while most want their girlfriend to be in shape, "too thin" does not turn heads the way normal, athletic, or voluptuous does.

✳ Women really do look their best when they are at their natural weight. The body assumes a place on the scale that's right for your type and you look great at that weight. Going too far in either direction detracts from your appearance.

Once a BC Babe comes to these realizations, she's ready to move out of the I-want-to-be-perfect state of mind and on to a more normal, balanced way of living. She buys a few pairs of black pants in case she gains a pound or two, gives her diet books to a friend, and breathes a sigh of relief that her days as an extreme workout queen are over for good.

Long-Term Living

As a BC Babe, you learn that you just can't sustain an extreme fitness routine forever. But just because you end up back in reality doesn't mean you have to give up completely on being healthy. You can find a middle ground, one you can live with that doesn't require banning all bread, undergoing hypnosis, or eating two bags of carrots a day while standing on your head. When we enter into a mode of extreme dieting and fitness, we make short-term changes we can't possibly stick to, instead of doing the little things each day to change our lives and get into better shape for the long haul. But the little things are far more effective and easy to do. Give some of them a try.

I've been on a constant diet for the last two decades. I've lost a total of 789 pounds. By all accounts, I should be hanging from a charm bracelet.

Erma Bombeck

Little Changes in Eating Habits

Dealing with the presence of food in your life can be challenging and tiring if you're trying to watch every morsel you eat. Given that so much of life revolves around food, how can you restrict yourself and still go on living normally? You really can't. You can, however, safeguard against overdoing it without putting in so much thought and effort that it becomes an obsession. How?

* Eat a snack before you go out to dinner or the grocery store. Never enter a major food situation hungry, because you risk going overboard and consuming everything in sight.
* Drink hot beverages. Tea can make you feel full, so when you have the urge to eat late at night, try having a cup of tea instead. Drink a hot beverage with your meal as well, because it will fill you up faster.
* Don't ignore the obvious. Eating more good things that are low in fat, such as vegetables, will keep you satisfied. Eat breakfast in the morning and eat small meals throughout the day instead of large ones. By doing so, you keep your blood sugar steady and you crave less junk throughout the day. Try this for two months and see what happens.

Food is like sex: when you abstain, even the worst stuff begins to look good.

Beth McCollister

✳ Buy less junk. If you don't have cookies or chips on your countertop, you certainly can't eat them. If you do buy them, get a smaller bag. The less junk you have around, the easier it will be to resist.

✳ Read the fine print or at least be aware of the sales pitch behind a lot of low-fat, low-carb foods. Just because something says it is good for you does not mean that it really is. In the end, the key to staying in shape is to burn more calories than you consume, regardless of where those calories come from.

✳ Eat small pieces of chocolate or your dessert of choice regularly. Don't deprive yourself completely of the foods you love because if you do, you're going to lose it one day and down an entire box of Cadbury bars. If you eat junk occasionally, you won't feel deprived.

Exercise

You don't have to run the Boston Marathon to stay in shape. Go to the gym and put your best foot forward, but don't kill yourself on the treadmill. Remember that doing something, however small, is better than not exercising at all. If you don't have time to work out every day, do little things to burn extra calories.

✳ Walk with a friend instead of going out to dinner to catch up.

✳ Walk when you run errands instead of taking your car.

✳ Get a dog so you're forced to go outside regularly.

✳ Visit people in person at work instead of calling them from down the hall.

✳ And everyone's favorite . . . take the stairs. But let's face it, who really wants to take the stairs at work in the morning? Get on the elevator and just walk an extra block at night.

Other Habits

You can also make basic lifestyle changes to help you maintain a healthy, balanced approach to food and fitness. Try some of the following:

* Buy clothes that fit. Don't buy the smaller size hoping you'll fit into it (even though it is a tough temptation to resist). Buy clothes that feel right on you and make you look good today. Don't postpone dressing the way you want to dress in the hopes that you'll lose that extra five pounds.

* Hang out with people who have a healthy attitude about their bodies. Help those friends who take their diet and exercise too far to learn the principle of moderation. Don't become like them but instead be a role model for normal eating and a healthy body image.

* Stay busy. It's pretty hard to eat too much when you're busy doing things you enjoy that involve your hands. Play tennis, lift weights, or do something crafty. Keep your days full and you'll resist the urge to snack.

This "little things every day" mentality can help a former BC Babe live a happy, satisfying life while still maintaining her health and looks. Take small steps toward your goals, steps that you can repeat consistently without pressure and pain. Ditch the life-changing resolutions that never end up being very life-changing anyway.

When your time as a BC Babe is over, you'll feel committed to having a more realistic view of your body and adopting lifelong habits that are sustainable in lieu of quick fixes. Instead of spending your time trying to become perfect, you'll focus on being your own personal best, exercising in moderation, and eating normally. Ultimately, you'll leave the BC Babe phase behind but will maintain your health and happiness.

When I buy cookies I eat just four and throw the rest away. But first I spray them with Raid so I won't dig them out of the garbage later. Be careful, though, because that Raid really doesn't taste that bad.

Janette Barber

Real-Life Tales from BC Babes

66I was obsessed with getting in shape and finding a new funkier hairstyle. I had my hairdresser cut layers all over my head and I cried for three months until it grew out. 99

66When I was in college, I woke up every morning at 5:45 religiously and ran five miles. What was I thinking? 99

66If I broke down and ate chocolate when I was on my diet, it was like the human vacuum cleaner was unleashed. I would use that moment of weakness as a license to eat everything in sight. 99

66I look back at those times when I thought I was fat, and I never looked that bad. I don't know what was going through my head. 99

66I still think the best way to look good is to wear nylons under your pants. They hold everything in. 99

❝ I have tried every product on the market that says "Look your best" on the packaging—home perms, sunless tanner, "hair power" vitamins, you name it. It's all in my bathroom collecting dust. ❞

❝ No matter how much I exercise, I always get tired walking up the stairs. It's so bizarre how certain movements use muscles you didn't even know you had. ❞

❝ I've spent my entire life pledging to "start tomorrow." Finally I realized I'm never going to start a diet tomorrow. I just have to start doing little things every day. ❞

thechameleon
i'll have what he's having

the chameleon at a glance

nickname
[Insert name]'s girlfriend

look
Her boyfriend's look; he bought a surfer necklace so she did too.

fashion
Shorts with his college logo on them; the same dress his best female friend has.

phrases
"What are you having?" "What are you wearing?" "What are you ordering?"

love interest
Her new beau, placed high upon a pedestal.

favorite songs
Tunes she never heard before she met him.

events/activities
Anything he likes to do.

friends
Her boyfriend, his friends, his friends' girlfriends, that's all.

life goal
To marry him and live happily ever after.

Mountain-climber man loves hiking so his girlfriend trades in her strappy sandals for rugged wear. Three weeks later she's climbing Kilimanjaro, inhaling trail mix, and sleeping under the stars. Banker boy is addicted to his work/gym routine so she joins him, staying late at the office and hitting the treadmill religiously for six months straight. If you ever altered part or all of yourself to become more like your latest beau, you have been through the Chameleon phase.

A Chameleon morphs into the man she's dating, turning her back on her brunette roots because he likes blonds or skydiving with Adventure Dude after a lifetime of fearing the upper bunk. It is not that she doesn't have her own interests or needs. In fact, she has plenty of opinions but something in her brain switches off her stronger self when she meets a guy she adores. She kisses her own interests goodbye and adopts his because he's so much fun.

The Chameleon phase can leave a girl feeling as though she's living life on a stage, changing costumes constantly to play a new part. Her boyfriend becomes the center of her universe because he's so darn cute and makes her heart go "thump." The good news is that after a girl goes through this morphing process enough times, she realizes it needs to stop and decides that doing her own thing isn't so bad after all. She becomes determined to hold on to part of herself regardless of who she's dating. But until this epiphany occurs, she meets men and enjoys living in their world for a while. She becomes a Chameleon.

Whether you're a Chameleon now or you were at one point in your past, this chapter will help you laugh at this phase and celebrate it. Then you'll learn to leave it behind for good and move on to brighter, more independent days.

Me-Metamorphosis

Are you a Chameleon? A Chameleon changes her looks or her body to please her latest beau, or goes to great lengths to learn an activity that he enjoys. Sometimes the changes are obvious; she trades in her conservative suit for leather and lace. Other changes are subtle swings of her personality, moods, or friendships. Not all changes we make in our relationships are bad. Obviously some level of compromise is required to make a union work. But the Chameleon takes compromise a little too far and does some funny, crazy things she would never normally do.

Review the following possible forms of me-metamorphosis to determine whether or not you've ever been a Chameleon.

The Look He Loves

You start lifting weights because your beau likes girls who are buff. You wax your eyebrows into a surprised look because he thinks it's sexy. When he makes a comment about which dress looks good on you, you take it to heart and declare him the ultimate makeover maven. If you're a Chameleon with your looks, you do things like:

✳ Cut your locks short because he says he loves pixie types.
✳ Purchase the new, funky green pants he pointed out in a catalog.

✳ Wear khakis and a white polo to fit in with him on the golf course.

✳ Agree to get the back tattoo he thinks is sexy.

✳ Wear less makeup because he prefers girls who are "natural."

✳ Give up your heels because he wants to feel taller when he's with you.

✳ Wear the feather-laden lingerie he admired in the Victoria's Secret window.

His Purchases

You never realized how much you adore classic rock until you started hanging out with your favorite guy. In fact, you're still not sure you like it entirely, but you are getting used to it and you bought three CDs to help you along. He seems to know just which music, DVDs, electronic gadgets, and other household items to buy, so you follow suit and make a few purchases too. On the road to Chameleon, you do things like:

✳ Buy a Nautica striped shower curtain similar to his and throw out your floral one.

✳ Purchase South American mambo music because he listens to it in his car.

✳ Invest in the MP3 player he swears "no human being can live without."

✳ Get hooked on fine Chianti because he has five bottles on his wine rack.

✳ Splurge on a high-definition TV because he told you to "get with the times."

His Activities

You wouldn't normally spend your vacation hang-gliding in the Alps, parasailing in the Pacific, or trekking through the wilderness, but heck, you're game if cute boyfriend wants to take these trips. So you splurge on a pair of cute pink hiking boots and take off into the outback. Even though there are some things you'd rather be doing, you resolve to enjoy his activities and do things like:

* Sleep in a tent by the ocean even though you prefer a hotel room, or at the very least a pop-up camper.
* Meow like the girl on the cable access show because he says he loves her sex kitten routine.
* Let beer kegs and funnels reappear for your birthday bash because he thinks a party isn't a party without them.
* Overcome your fear of motorcycles by riding on the back of his for six hours in the rain.
* Join him for his 5 A.M. marathon training sessions even though you aren't a big fan of running (to say the least), or of getting up early, for that matter.

His Favorite Friends

You love your fabulous friends, but you just don't have as much time for them as you used to. You're working to play the part of the "cool new girlfriend," so you become the friendly Chameleon and do things like:

* Let his old college roommate sleep on your couch for a few months and drape his dirty clothes over your closet door.
* Ditch girls' night out (again) so you can watch the big basketball game with the boys.
* Become close to his friends' girlfriends even though you probably wouldn't hang out with them if you weren't linked by your boyfriends.
* Sign up for the people-relations seminar because his brother insists you're not nice enough.
* Play "mom" to his buddies, cooking them dinner before the game.

His Personality Preferences

Before you started dating him you were outspoken and assertive, but he prefers quiet girls so you try to zip your lip more often. He has an older-women fetish so you play up your sophisticated side. You always follow his lead, hoping to make the relationship better and keep your honey happy. You just want him to think you're as cool as you think he is. So you do what it takes to make him laugh, understand his point of view, and showcase your best side. If you're a Chameleon with your personality, you do things like:

* Cook lots of meals because he told you he likes homemaker types, even though your nickname used to be Takeout Queen.
* Laugh at his jokes and even repeat them despite the fact that you rarely get the punch line.
* Learn to go with the flow because he's laid back, even though you're naturally wired.
* Speak using his slang expressions, like "sweet" and "babe," despite the fact that they initially struck you as odd.
* Learn to keep quiet when his shows are on (okay, maybe you never go that far).

If you can relate to any of these changes, you might have undergone me-metamorphosis with a guy you dated. We're not talking just a little compromise here and there to keep your beau happy; we're talking bigger changes that make you forget some of the things that are important to you. A Chameleon forgets who she is for a while and becomes more and more like the man she adores. How does she end up in such a precarious position? Well, first of all, he's so cute! It's so hard not to want to make him happy. But there are other causes of me-metamorphosis. The next section will explore some of the reasons why we go through this phase.

● gaining perspective If someone you know well tells you that you're just not the same anymore now that you're dating your new guy, listen with a keen ear. The perceptive onlooker will notice you're becoming a Chameleon before you will and help you reclaim your sassy, independent self.

Behind the Mask

Why is it so darn easy to fall into the Chameleon trap? Even strong women do it. You don't have to be a mindless she-bot to lose yourself in a relationship, especially when you feel that the guy you're with is the love of your life. We morph into other people sometimes too. We are in a rut so we mimic a friend or coworker who seems to have it all together.

What prompts the Chameleon phase to kick in, and why do so many otherwise grounded women go through it? Any number of triggers can get the process started, leaving you in a state of me-metamorphosis.

His Twinkling Eyes

He's cute, he's smart, he's funny, and you are positive he's "the one." You are blinded by his twinkling eyes and mesmerizing smile. So what do you do? Everything you can to make this guy think the world of you!

When we are new to the dating scene, we think guys like us more when we become like them. Then after a while we realize, "Wait a minute! When I give guys a hard time, they find me more interesting." The moment we have this epiphany, we toss out the accommodating routine and move out of the Chameleon phase into "feisty girl" mode. Then we really start having fun.

The Shifty Self

It's not easy for a girl in today's world to figure out what she wants to do with her life and how she wants to live it.

Sometimes a guy falls into the mix right when you feel that you're in desperate need of direction. If he has all the answers, it seems easier to let him lead.

When the shifty self is responsible for your metamorphosis, you might find yourself following the leads of other people in your life too. You might dress like a friend because you don't trust your own fashion instincts, or copy your coworker's presentation format because you're unsure of how your own will fly.

No man was ever great by imitation.
Samuel Johnson

In its most benign form, a Chameleon's urge to follow might be caused by laziness. It requires less energy to adopt someone else's way of life than it does to define your own. And sometimes it's not so bad to seek someone else's advice or learn by imitating their style. But if you're living your life trying to be like others, obviously it's time to strike out on your own. Eventually you have to realize that what works for other people won't always work for you. You'll be happier if you build your own confidence and find your sassy self again.

Insecure Surroundings

You enter a graduate program, start a new job, or move to a different city and your life is filled with stress. You want to succeed and you want to fit in with new people you meet. On top of that, all of the changes make you rethink your direction in life. You question what job you want, where you want to live, and why you're on this earth to begin with. Then a boyfriend who's already comfortable with his world enters the equation. It just seems easier to follow his lead for a while. A girl who morphs for this reason will rarely take the time to figure out what she wants from her own life as long as he's around to rely upon. If you find yourself in this position, step back and put some energy into making your world what you want it to be before you move forward with him. You might not even like him anymore once you have your own butt in gear. Make sure you're not staying with a guy simply because he provides the security that you don't have the energy to find on your own.

Domineering Dude

This guy has a Messiah complex and criticizes everything about you. Or maybe he's not that blatant, but you get the feeling he expects you to make your boobs grow, your butt shrink, and your wardrobe include more items from trashy lingerie catalogs. Initially his demands seem benign, so you let him make the decisions, suggest outfits for you to wear, and comment on your cooking. But this guy gets annoying quickly because he continuously ups the ante. His demands grow more and more serious until you feel that you're surrounded by an electric fence. Domineering Dude can turn one of the most confident chicks into a weak woman, convincing her over time that he knows what's best for her. If you find that a guy like this is controlling your life, kick the bastard goodbye and make your world what you want it to be on your own.

The only good imitations are those that poke fun at bad originals.

François de La Rochefoucauld

The Postcrisis Morph

Someone close to you passes away, you just endured a horrible breakup, or you're experiencing an unexplainable state of depression. Because of the crisis you face, you feel more insecure than you've ever felt in your life. These major events steal every ounce of your energy, and all you really want to do is curl up in a ball and hide out from people and responsibilities. If a strong, centered guy comes along during this time, it's hard not to cling for dear life to the inner tube floating nearby. This type of morphing may be impossible to prevent and perhaps it is even therapeutic for a stint. When the crisis has passed, however, the "I am him" urge should go away too.

Scary Girl Stories

You hear guys you know talk about "the ball and chain" girlfriend and you're terrified to be her. So instead of risking scary girl status by being your cool, confident self, you go to the extreme to accommodate his every whim. You'd rather be an amoeba than be labeled "uncompromising psycho." But if you listen closely to the guys talk, you'll hear them make fun of pushovers too. You don't make headway in your love life by trying to please the opinionated peanut gallery. The reality is that you have to be yourself in every relationship. The right guy will like you for who you are whether you're sweet or spunky.

Buildup

It took you so long to meet someone you like that the last thing you want to do is screw it up. Dating is fun and exciting, but it can be tiring too. You've met guys at bars, clubs, the post office, the bank, the deli, and through a multitude of

● **voluntary morphing** Know the difference between voluntary and involuntary morphing. If a guy pressures you to change fundamental parts of yourself, run far away from him fast. Keep in mind that he probably won't be satisfied even if you do change. Guys pull this maneuver to gain power because they feel insecure. They are not really trying to make you a better person. If, however, you are behind your own metamorphosis, you can work to reclaim yourself while maintaining a relationship with your guy.

services. There was something about every one of them that just wasn't quite right. When you finally met this one, he had potential and you felt relieved. After jumping through so many hoops to get to this point in the relationship—awkward dinner date, phone calls, analyzing messages, interpreting his moves, dinner again—you have no intention of messing it up, so you morph. You decide that if you're going to keep this thing going and avoid returning to the market, you've got to make him happy.

Dating Pressure

Sometimes a girl will try hard to make a bad relationship work because she feels pressure to be dating someone, anyone, and doesn't want to live life solo again. There's something nice about having a warm body to come home to on a Friday night, a person to call when you're bored, and someone to share the details of the day with. You might feel pressure to keep the wrong guy around if:

* A string of nights out with bad dates who pick their teeth and burp at the table leaves you certain the new guy is worth marrying immediately.
* The "his and hers" bathrobe advertisement makes you feel that you should be settling down sooner rather than later.
* The fifth horrendous bridesmaid dress you have to buy makes you really eager to return the favor by making your friends wear lime green hoop gowns.
* The reflection of your bare arms in a department store mirror leaves you certain no man alive will look your way again other than the one you're now dating, who knew you prepoundage.
* You can't get the lid off the pickles by yourself . . . again.

✳ You can't figure out how to use half the tools in the tool-box under your sink.

✳ You're tired of installing the air conditioner by yourself every spring.

The desire to have a date for weddings and parties can make a girl work to keep a relationship going even if the guy is a loser. It's easier to learn to love Pink Floyd's "The Wall" than to push the wrong guy over one. So she sticks it out and becomes more like him to make the relationship work.

Keep in mind that the better you know someone, the easier it is to open up and be yourself around that person. It's normal to be a Chameleon with strangers because you don't know where you stand with them yet. Sometimes we accommodate people until we get a feel for which jokes, views, and attitudes we can get away with. Eventually, if we're not comfortable around them, we minimize contact.

If you've been dating someone for a few months and you still feel like you're playing the "get to know you" game, the relationship is not right. You should never feel as if you have to be someone else when you're around the guy you adore. A relationship is not only about how he treats you. It's also about who you are when you're with him. And for it to work, you have to be an even happier version of the real you when he's by your side.

If love means that one person absorbs the other, then no real relationship exists any more. Love evaporates; there is nothing left to love. The integrity of self is gone.

Ann Oakley

The Pros and Cons of Morphing

As a Chameleon, you lose yourself temporarily, but you can't hide your true self forever. Eventually you bounce back to being yourself and you're much smarter for the wear. You might look back on this phase and think, "Why in the world did I let that happen? I am so fabulous on my own." When you examine the process closely, however, you see that you did learn valuable lessons from morphing into the men you adored, and those lessons alone make the experience worthwhile.

Lesson #1: The Chameleon Learns to Appreciate Her Independence Even More

When you completely and utterly lose yourself for a while, you certainly appreciate your confidence and individuality when you get it back. The Chameleon reclaims herself through a process that goes something like this.

Step 1: She expands her horizons and tries new things.

When lust and love are involved, a chick will bungee jump from the Empire State Building if that's what the guy wants her to do. She'll eat weird foods, call in sick once a week, inner-tube down the Hudson, or join the Peace Corps. A hot guy saying "jump" can make even the most independent-minded woman ask "how high?" and then open the airplane door and nosedive. Is there anything you've done in your life only because the guy you dated made you do it, or because you wanted to appease him, impress him, or just have fun with him? Once you remember these things, appreciate that guy (even if you can't stand him now) because he broadened your interests and contributed some variety and spice to your life.

Step 2: She regains consciousness, defines herself, and declares her own likes and dislikes.

Even if she does jump from the plane or put forth a damn good effort to become part of his trapeze act, eventually she realizes that these things don't feel natural to her.

But every now and then, a guy will introduce her to something she sticks with. Maybe she never knew she could sing until her karaoke-loving boyfriend dragged her to pub nights, where she could belt out tunes on the microphone. Nevertheless, more often than not a Chameleon ends up realizing that she's doing things she doesn't want to do and being someone she's not. She starts to appreciate the fact that she loves to dance and doesn't want to stop doing it just because her boyfriend refuses to join her. She appreciates those parts of herself that are unique, the parts he doesn't "get," and she makes a conscious decision to get back to living life her way.

Step 3: She ditches her chameleon tendencies and asserts herself.

The Chameleon pledges to date men who appreciate her for who she is. She's had enough biking and hiking. She's ready to reclaim her weekends, do her own thing, and let her boyfriend do his. She knows she can't live her life being someone she's not. So she stops trying to make it work with men who aren't right for her, and instead dates guys who think that her real self, the one who prefers shoes to blues, is fabulous. She makes an effort to maintain those things that are important to her even when she's in a fantastic relationship with a guy she adores.

Trying to live a life that's not in line with your natural personality or interests is exhausting. It requires a lot of work to try to convince yourself that you love tennis, travel, and spicy foods if you want to stay home, read, and eat ice cream. If you love kids and he can't stand the little munchkins, or he wants to hike and you are allergic to every plant in the universe, these issues will constantly be a problem.

● relationship review All relationships involve work and compromise, but when your relationship becomes constant work and you are surrendering yourself regularly to make him happy, it is time to move on.

Most women go through the Chameleon phase with more than one man before they realize they are doing this little morphing routine. Eventually a girl senses that her relationships don't feel right because she isn't being herself in them. Then she declares her independence, and begins to appreciate more than ever those parts of herself that make her unique. When you finally ditch the Chameleon phase for good, you hold on to the memory of how easy it was to lose yourself in a relationship, and that makes you work even harder to maintain your independence and individuality.

Lesson #2: The Chameleon Has a New Understanding of Men
Aside from learning lessons about yourself and what you want out of life, as a Chameleon you'll also acquire a deeper understanding of what makes men tick. Not even reading every guy-guide on the planet could teach you what you'll learn from experience. New knowledge of male habits, preferences, faults, and foibles is yours because you are, in essence, him—without the body hair of course. By putting yourself in his shoes, you see the world from the male point of view and learn just what you'll be dealing with forever (yikes!) if you decide to stick it out with one of these odd creatures. You learn things like these:

✳ Most men are "cutesier" than they'll admit.
　✓ He refers to his shamrock-covered shorts as his "Shammys."
　✓ He cradles the dog like a baby when you're not looking.

✳ Men have no concept of pain.
- ✓ He thinks shaving is tough even though he only has to do his chin.
- ✓ He doesn't understand that giving birth is different from going to the bathroom.

✳ Men are as sensitive as women are about their weight.
- ✓ He insists that his waist size is a 33 until you explain to him that the pants need to be moved up *over* his spare tire.
- ✓ If you suggest that he gets a salad at dinner, he snaps, "Why? Do I need to cut calories?"

✳ Men appreciate independent women with opinions.
- ✓ He lost his ability to pick out his clothes on his own and is thrilled when you do it for him.
- ✓ He quickly mastered the response "Whatever you want, honey."

✳ Men like to call themselves athletes even if they never play.
- ✓ He refers to his colleagues as his "team" and his accomplishments as "touchdowns" even though his feet haven't been on AstroTurf in a decade.
- ✓ He can offer commentary on every pro basketball move as if he wrote the game book.

✳ Men are delusional about their own health habits.
- ✓ He washes down his low-carb dinner with dark-brewed beer and sugary soda.
- ✓ He swears that an article he read said cheesy nachos are healthy because of the spices.

✳ Men love to feel useful.
- ✓ You tell him you can carry the box on your own and he insists you submit to a bench-press challenge to prove you can do it.
- ✓ You put him to work assembling the IKEA cabinet and he starts calling himself Mr. Fix-it.

✳ Men have a short attention span and no memory.
   ✓ He channel surfs with the remote and thinks five
   minutes on "your program" is generous.
   ✓ You tell him 100 times that you're going to the grocery store and he still can't remember where you are
   when your sister calls.
✳ All men have some annoying quality.
   ✓ He sniffles like he's immersed in a tube full of pollen
   or laughs like the worst sitcom laugh track in history.
   ✓ He leaves half a paper towel on the roll so he doesn't
   have to change it.

As a Chameleon, you learn firsthand what makes men tick,
and though you might not ever fully relate to his desire to watch
twenty-five basketball games in a row, you'll at least know
enough about his schedule to plan a shopping trip when they
are on. When he becomes the center of your universe, you have
a front-row view of the way his world works. This knowledge of
the male mind is priceless.

Lesson #3: The Chameleon Sees the World Through Someone Else's Eyes

Every man you morph into teaches you to appreciate different things about the world. Mr. Artist explains the deep meaning behind the blotched color ensemble he has hanging on his
bedroom wall. Mr. Metrosexual teaches you new techniques in
skin care. Unemployed Guy gives you a greater appreciation for
a steady paycheck.

The Chameleon phase can be an educational, meaningful
time in a woman's life. You will forever after remember the things
you learned from the different types of men you dated. . . .

Granola (Outdoor) Guy

He showed you the difference between poison and edible berries. He took you on hikes up mountains you never knew existed to peaks with breathtaking views. You'll probably never again spend time sleeping under the stars like you did with Granola Guy.

The Rapper Wannabe

Slim Shady was just a blond kid flashing across the TV screen until you dated Rapper Wannabe. He gave you a new appreciation for music that you just didn't understand before you dated him. Now you find yourself humming a hip-hop beat when you're in the car.

"Between Jobs" Joe

He made you feel like you're a superstar because you hold down a full-time job. You never felt so together as you did when you were dating "Between Jobs" Joe. With him by your side you felt utterly relaxed because no matter how bad you screwed up, at least you had a job.

The Money Maverick

He had a portfolio that put Charles Schwab to shame. He watched the markets every day and followed certain stocks like they were his babies. Your idea of investing was sticking a few dollars in the bank before you started dating him. Now you are on track to retire at 40.

The Dude from Abroad

Your knowledge of other countries was severely lacking and your dinners consisted of hamburgers and fries before you dated Dude from Abroad. Suddenly you dined on foreign delicacies and talked about global politics. He expanded your view of the world, taught you a few interesting words in French, and you've never been quite the same since.

Cowboy Chris

He grew up in a place where cows and horses are abundant, or at least he wishes he did. He loves country music and uses terms like "Howdy." He even called you "Little Lady" once and you were so enamored that you didn't even raise an eyebrow. He taught you to appreciate a good Western, a good steak, and most of all, a simple way of life. You still enjoy a top-forty country tune now and then.

Everywhere, we learn only from those whom we love.

Johann Wolfgang von Goethe

Workplace Buddy

You skipped meetings and called in sick until you had a Workplace Buddy. Then you arrived at 8 A.M. energized and ready for the day ahead. He taught you that a lot can be communicated by kicks under a conference table and that no project is a dull project if you're working on it with someone you like. Most important, you learned from him that breaking up in close quarters is no fun at all.

Ambiguous Man

You still aren't sure if you were dating him or if he was a telemarketer who wouldn't stop calling you. You went out with him on occasion, suffered through his confusing signals, and finally decided he just wasn't worth the trouble anymore. At the time you wanted to strangle him, but now you realize that he taught you to draw the line fast when a relationship isn't working. Thanks to him, you finally learned to cut men out of your life quickly if they aren't treating you well.

The Creative Chef

You couldn't name three types of mushrooms before you met the Creative Chef. Within weeks of dating him you could identify all the spices in your spice rack and you knew how to use a meat thermometer. You also made a mean soufflé more than once with his help.

The Self-Assured Guy

Whatever insecurities you had he helped you push aside, not only by being supportive but also by being self-confident. Through watching him tackle the world with enthusiasm, you learned to do the same.

There is no dependence that can be sure but a dependence upon one's self.

John Gay

The Sports Buff

You might have to wrack your brain to figure out what all those nights you spent watching games at pubs really taught you about life. But if nothing else, the Sports Buff is always the first to call a group together for a pregame party, so you picked up some knowledge about chips and dips. With Sports Buff in your dating history, you will never again feel as if the guy you're with is sports-obsessed. His interest in the game will always seem mild by comparison.

Each man you date does bring something new to your life. Sometimes you simply learn painful lessons that make your relationships better the next time around. Other times you experience wonderful parts of the world that you would never have experienced otherwise. So remember the men you dated fondly, try to identify the contributions they made to your life, and hold on to the lessons you learned.

Lesson #4: The Chameleon Commits to Improving Her Relationships

Eventually you realize that you have to stop making such extreme compromises in your relationships. You realize how extraordinary and unique you really are, so you resolve to take back your life and celebrate your individuality. From this point forward, the men you date must appreciate you for who you are or hit the road. You make promises to yourself like these:

❋ You will never give up on your own interests and activities, because being true to yourself makes your relationships stronger.

❋ You will wait for the right guy—the one who loves those things about you that make you unique.

❋ You will not attempt to fit in with the guy you're dating by wearing things that make you uncomfortable and listening to music you dislike.

❋ You'll believe in who you are, hold on to those things that are important to you, and make an effort to have an independent life even when you're in a great relationship.

● **what men want** Men say that they enjoy dating women who have their own interests and activities. They like women with confidence and spunk. So give that guy some attitude and celebrate your own style.

During your stint as a Chameleon, you realize that you do need to give a little in a relationship, but giving too much is just as bad as not giving at all. In the end, you'll be able to say goodbye to this phase for good and move on to a more confident state of mind.

I have an everyday religion that works for me. Love yourself first, and everything else falls into line.

Lucille Ball

Flying High

Once a girl is finished for good with me-metamorphosis, she is happier and more content than she ever was before. She knows that there are certain parts of herself that she just won't compromise. Her interests and beliefs make her who she is. She realizes that certain men, even great men, might not be the right fit for her, and that she has to hold out for the one with whom she really clicks.

So like a butterfly, the Chameleon goes through me-metamorphosis and comes out new and improved. She has a deeper knowledge of what she wants out of life, who she is, and where she's going. This knowledge allows her to fly high even when she's flying solo.

Cherish forever what makes you unique, 'cuz you're really a yawn if it goes.

Bette Midler

Signs That You're Flying High

It's easy to compromise in a relationship without going too far once you make a commitment to remain true to yourself, your needs, and your values. You'll know you are no longer capable of becoming a Chameleon when:

- You can understand your boyfriend's perspective and even empathize with his "fight the beer tax" campaign, without obliterating your own beliefs and interests.
- You state aloud to your outdoorsy boyfriend that no life jacket, regardless of how expensive or large it is, will ever make you a fan of white-water rafting.
- You give in and let him buy the taco mix he wants without feeling that he always gets his own way. You know which battles to fight and which to let him win.
- You've been dating someone for three months and you still go out with your friends at least once a week.
- You meet a wonderful, adorable stud but the two of you can't agree on anything. You let him go, knowing you'll meet a better guy down the road.
- You see other women in their Chameleon phase and long to relay to them the lessons you learned from going through it yourself.
- You feel great on your own and you view a guy as a nice addition to your life, not a necessity.
- You never feel the urge to settle for less than what you deserve.
- When you finally meet the right guy, your gut instincts tell you it's working and you feel that you are truly yourself around him.

When you're flying high you know that relationships aren't supposed to be so overwhelming that you don't recognize yourself when you're in them. You have newfound knowledge of what it means to make compromises and how that differs from losing yourself completely. With this gem of genius, you can go forth with a stronger sense of self and maintain your superstar sass whether or not there's a man in your life.

When the Chameleon phase is over, a girl often feels nostalgic remembering the men she left behind because they were such a big part of her life for a while. She realizes that when she dated them she knew them better than she knew herself. She looks back on the things guys convinced her to do—trying escargot, walking on the rope ladder across the ravine, or dyeing her hair platinum blond—and she laughs at the part of herself that was so gullible and eager to please. She doesn't remember this phase as a "a waste of time," but instead remembers it fondly. She cherishes the crazy experiences she never would have had otherwise. Her Chameleon phase may have been challenging but she knows it contributed in many ways to the wiser, more confident woman she is today.

Remember always that you not only have the right to be an individual, you have an obligation to be one.

Eleanor Roosevelt

Real-Life Tales from Chameleons

66 I lied to my boyfriend and told him I love mountain biking because he does. Big mistake. He figured out pretty quickly on our first ride together that I'm not exactly an outdoorsy type of girl. 99

66 I stopped wearing makeup because my boyfriend didn't like it. Think "Casper" and you'll have an image of me at that time. I looked like a corpse. 99

66 I swear to this day that I only work on Wall Street because my college boyfriend took a job in finance and I wanted to be like him, so I followed. 99

66 I baked cookies almost every week for this guy I was dating because he liked "homemaker types." I found out eventually that he was sharing them at work with a girl he was cheating on me with. My new boyfriend bakes cookies for me. 99

66 I bought a down comforter because he had one on his bed. The first night he slept over, he broke out in hives. I found out his was imitation down, because he's allergic to the real thing. 99

66 I bought my boyfriend's mother a case of meat marinades as a housewarming gift because he told me she "loves to grill." Turned out he meant "grill" as in ask a lot of questions. I also found out later that she is a vegetarian. 99

chapter 7

thecrisischick
junk food and sleep

the crisis chick at a glance

nickname
PMS Girl, Queen of Confusion

look
Pale, broken out, tired, and depressed.

fashion
The same stretchy jeans and T-shirt every day for a month.

phrase
"Ugh, what am I going to do with my life?"

love interest
Absolutely no one but her beloved pet.

favorite songs
Slow, sappy love songs.

events/activities
Sleep, eat, sleep more, and sometimes shower.

friends
Her mother and sister or anyone else so close to her that they can tolerate her moodiness, lend an ear, and expect nothing in return.

life goal
"Stop asking me or I'm going to slit my wrists."

She's living her life in a rhythmic fashion—work, gym, TV, sleep; work, gym, TV, sleep—and then one morning she gets a call: "Your little sister is getting married!" or "Your cousin just got promoted to senior executive at her company." And it makes her think "What the heck am I doing with MY life? I don't really like my job. I'm not sure if this guy is right for me, or if any guy is right for me, and I feel like a blob." She crawls into bed and sleeps the rest of the day away. When she awakens she doesn't feel much better. She is the Crisis Chick.

Whether it's a quarter-life crisis or an "I'm turning 30" crisis, it occurs somewhere before middle age and after adolescent hell on earth. It is a time when a girl should be excited about the future, planning for her career, her wedding, children, or whatever she dreams about for her life. But she's not. Instead, she's confused and sort of depressed too. She goes through the motions every day and thanks her lucky stars for the night-shift cleaning man, her only steady male admirer. She prays the paper shredder will soon catch her pant leg and take her life.

Faced with mixed messages about how she should be living, the Crisis Chick feels burdened when she has to decide which road to take. When she does choose, she fears she's leaving better paths behind. She looks at what other people are doing and evaluates herself against their progress, becoming increasingly confused about what she wants and what will make her happy.

The Crisis phase is an overwhelming time, but armed with the right tools, a girl can turn this phase into one that works for her. After much soul-searching, she can make a choice: Stay depressed or move ahead and take the steps necessary to make her life better. This chapter will help you do the latter. By giving you concrete ways to overcome your blues, you will learn how to turn your life into an exciting adventure and ditch the Crisis Chick phase for good.

Inside the Swirling Cyclone

Are you in the Crisis phase? Life inside the swirling cyclone of moods and madness is tough. For extended periods of time a Crisis Chick just doesn't want to get out of bed. When she does wake up she goes through the motions, and when she gets to work she can't remember how she got there because there is absolutely no variation in her routine any day of the week. She knows rationally that her life is not that bad, but she still feels ugly, exhausted, and in a rut. She chats with friends, watches people on television, and overhears coworkers talk about their more glamorous lives. Ultimately she determines that she is the only person on the planet who doesn't have a life plan.

Does this sound like you? If so, you might be in your Crisis Chick phase. Pay attention to other warning signs.

● **thirty-three is the new thirty** Men and women everywhere no longer have to dread the big 3-0. People graduate from school later, get married later, and everything in life seems pushed back a bit for this generation. So 33 is the new 30 and 30 is, well, more like 27.

Everything Is Wrong

A Crisis Chick has a problem everywhere she turns. There's a power outage when she's riding the subway in ninety-degree heat. Someone sideswipes her car. An old man tells her off when she bumps into him and her best friend sounds snotty on the phone. She isn't sure if things are really wrong or if they just seem wrong. Regardless, she can't wait to down a bottle of Prozac and get out of this phase.

She Meets No Worthwhile Guys to Date

She goes out with guy after guy but they are all major duds. Or she has a boyfriend but she just isn't sure if he's the right one. Dating is completely exhausting, more of a chore than a leisure activity. She can't figure out why Mr. Right doesn't just appear at her front door ready and willing to give her a back rub.

Doubt is the beginning, not the end, of wisdom.

George Iles

The World Is Against Her

She asks her dog for a kiss and he sniffs her a little and then sticks his nose up in the air. Minutes later she sees him licking his rear end. She drives to the store and the person in front of her drives twenty miles an hour until she lays on the horn. Then she flips the guy the bird and passes him only to find out the next day that it was her boss. She sits in the seat reserved for the elderly on the bus and an old lady with a cane chews her out for it. There is a line for every ladies' room she tries to use within a 100-mile radius.

Her Timing Is Off

The company BBQ is scheduled for the day she's out on vacation. She hurries to get to her doctor's appointment and has

Technology: Friend or Foe?

Technology is supposed to help a girl connect to other people in her times of need. But does technology help her solve her problems or just make her life more miserable? During crisis mode it can seem that blinking streetlights are spelling out "you suck" in Morse code. Technology seems to make crisis mode worse, and that's why a Crisis Chick dreams of moving to a hut on the beach. During crisis mode:

- You call the customer service center for a simple answer and end up navigating the world's largest voice mail system for more than an hour before getting disconnected.
- Hundreds of digital channels all seem to be playing movies or shows about happy, rich people in love.
- The Internet porn site you accidentally clicked on won't let you leave and stalks you all day with pop-ups.
- Your luggage ends up 3,000 miles away because of a problem with the new tracking system.
- An e-mail glitch sends your extremely personal message to everyone in your company.
- The microwave starts up every time you try to program the clock.
- The girl sitting next to you on the train blabs on her cell phone about the plans for her million-dollar wedding when you have cramps and a headache.

to sit for an hour in the waiting room once she gets there. She misses the wedding ceremony because she's caught in traffic. Whether she's trying to make it to an important event or get out of bed on time in the morning, she can't seem to get her life into sync with the rising and setting of the sun. She's too late or too early for everything.

She Hates Her Job

She goes into work every day and suffers through the same monotonous routine. She is angry with herself for enjoying the stability because she knows it is not challenging enough for her. She thought she would be a superstar by now and yet she's still getting paid less than her 16-year-old brother, who started his own Web design company from his bedroom. She can't even bring herself to look at job sites online because the whole process seems so overwhelming. Every career newsletter that pops up in her inbox makes her sick to her stomach.

She Sees Signs That She's Becoming Someone She Doesn't Want to Be

She wears stretch pants, sneakers, and big sweatshirts to hide her body from the world. She carries a recycled shopping bag to work every day. She is too tired and lazy to update her wardrobe or throw out the shoes with the heels worn off. She feels bitchy so she yells at kids playing nearby for being too loud. On occasion she acts like one of the older ladies she hated as a kid. She is mortified when she realizes she is starting to look like her mother.

Other People Seem Perfect

Another woman walks in the room and Crisis Chick immediately feels like the ugly stepchild. Her mind invents scenarios of what other women's lives are like. She imagines her coworker at age five winning the good prize at the amusement park and recalls how she always got stuck with the plastic spider ring. She imagines that her cousin in college is fighting off admiring guys. Crisis Chick determines that she is just not worthy of happiness and love like other women are.

Her World Is Disorganized

Every drawer in her apartment is a junk drawer and she doesn't have the energy to clean things up. The laundry pile is touching the ceiling and the bathtub has visible rings. She can find every receipt for everything she's ever purchased except the

● pep & patience When you're in Crisis Chick mode, it might feel as if other people are painfully annoying and their problems aren't anywhere near as bad as yours are. Though you may be right, try your hardest to be patient with friends, family, and coworkers during this time. Snapping at the people in your life will make things worse, not better.

receipt for the one item of clothing she really wants to return. She can locate every odd and end but she can't find the one piece of plastic she needs to make herself a cup of coffee with the new coffeemaker.

Her Brain Feels Like It Is Going to Explode from Analyzing Life

She has charts, graphs, schedules, and notebooks full of ideas. She has assessed what she wants to do with her life every which way. She's outlined the pros and cons of each option, purchased books on finding herself, and begged friends for advice, but she still isn't sure what she should be doing. She feels like she's made no progress in her current field or her love life despite all the years she's spent putting her best foot forward. She contemplates moving to Thailand to teach English or adopting a child or maybe just getting a cat. Any way she looks at her life, she just can't decide what in this world will really make her happy.

She Does Odd Things

She spends endless hours surfing the Web and tells her life story to strangers in chat rooms. She starts playing the guitar, gets a tattoo, and moves to a hut on the beach. Or she simply decides to revamp her look, dyeing her hair a reddish hue and purchasing the retro dress and platform heels she saw in a magazine. In extreme cases, she has an urge to experiment with her sexuality or travel the world with a guy she met online.

She Gets Really into Spiritual Stuff

She thinks about trying to live off the land for a year and she looks for signs from the heavens to point her in the right direction. She gets really interested in books and shows about philosophy and science and considers converting to a religion she's been reading about. She becomes convinced that she's been reincarnated or that the human race began with aliens that arrived during the time of the Egyptians. She makes an appointment to see an astrologer, a psychic, or anyone who can read her palm and tarot cards.

If several of these situations ring true to you, you are in the Crisis Chick phase. If you are experiencing them all at the same time, sound the red-alert alarm and keep reading.

What bothers me is the fact that I own the latest picture cell phone that does everything shy of having sex with me, it costs fifty bucks a month, and only one person calls me.

Anonymous

She Considers Reinventing Herself, from Scratch

She sees other women whose lives are different from her own and she considers momentarily reinventing herself to be more like one of them. If she's a business executive, she decides to become a teacher. If she's a teacher, she decides to go back to school and become a lawyer. Any dramatic change in lifestyle seems more appealing than what she's doing today. Soon, possible identities she never even considered before begin to look good:

The Rich Wife

Find a great guy with a nice fat paycheck, trade in the hectic daily grind for an apron, and spend the rest of her life dusting and baking like those housewives in the commercials. Or better yet, go to the spa all day and hire someone else to do the dusting. For a second, it seems like a divine plan. Then she meets that rich guy who snorts during dinner and she realizes she can't spend two seconds with him, let alone a lifetime. She talks to her stay-at-home sister, who says it's not all it's cracked up to be when the kids are sick and the dog is barking. Soon she's back to making her own life work.

The Save the World Woman

Quit her corporate job, fly to Zimbabwe, feed the hungry, and clothe the naked. Or at least work for a nonprofit, where she hears the lifestyle is easier and the days are more relaxed. She's ready to hand in her resignation when she reads an article about the nonprofit attorney working around the clock to defend the immigrants from Cuba. She realizes that maybe their lifestyle isn't that much better and maybe her heart is not in it after all. She resolves to spend a few more hours each week volunteering for a cause before she commits her life to it.

The Country Chick

Move to Iowa or Idaho or anywhere with ample open space to build a log cabin. Live off the land, grow a garden, and tend livestock. Or get a job in a mom-and-pop store nearby and chat

Look alive. Here comes a buzzard.
Lady Stella Reading

Tips from a Professional Loner

Feeling like you just need some time away to sort through your thoughts? Want to avoid human interaction for a while? Take some tips from a professional loner (but remember to put a limit to your time alone and reconnect with others once you're feeling refreshed).

- Stand in the far corner of the elevator so the annoying guy who's approaching can't see that you are in there. Let the door close. Woops, he can get the next one.
- Leave work early. Drape your coat over the back of your chair and put papers all over your desk, giving it that "temporarily stepped away" look.
- Get caller ID or use an answering machine to screen all calls.
- Park your car on another block so people think you're not home.
- Use e-mail as a preferred method of communication and leave on your out-of-office reply by "accident" so people don't expect a quick answer.
- Work on your "I don't see him standing there" facial expression so you can use it when someone you don't want to see is nearby.
- Tell everyone you are taking a two-week vacation out of the country and you'll talk to them when you get back.

with the regulars as they come in each day. It seems so simple that she's not sure why she didn't think of it before. Then she visits her friend in the country to get a feel for what her new life would be like. After forty-eight hours of searching for ways to fill her time, she realizes she needs a week, not a lifetime, away from the maddening crowds.

The Actress

Quit her day job, move to L.A., work as a bartender on the beach, and go on auditions. If all these other people can do it, so can she. She researches ways to get started, talks to people about the business, and realizes it might take more than a week or two before she gets that break and makes her screen debut. So she decides to take a few creative classes where she is and think of the actress thing as a long-term goal, not a quick fix.

The Global Overlord

Go back to school, get an M.B.A., a J.D., a Ph.D., and her C.P.A. certification. Find a job working for a *Fortune* 500 company and rise to power. Buy a yacht, a couple of dozen mansions, property in the Bahamas, and a collection of vintage wines. So she makes some phone calls, investigates a dozen academic programs, and talks to her significant other about the pros and cons of making a big switch. But when she hears about the outlay of cash for business school and the amount of time it takes to make it through, she reconsiders. She still might go that route, but decides that perhaps she should spend a little more time making the decision.

A Kid Again

Move back in with her parents, pay them minimal rent, and get a job closer to home. At least she would have the support of mom and dad nearby and the old familiar life she once loved. She packs up her bags and goes to visit her folks for a weekend, prepared to break the news that she's coming back. Her mom picks her up at the airport and chats her ear off in the car. Her dad puts her to work sanding a coffee table for the recreation room in the basement. She sleeps in her old bed and something about the mattress just doesn't feel right. Soon she realizes she loves her parents dearly, but moving home is definitely not the answer.

During the Crisis Chick phase everything in your life is just plain old wrong, and almost every alternative seems more appealing than the life you're in. You feel unattractive, unsuccessful, and unmotivated. On the contrary, life seems so simple for everyone around you. Certain that you are destined for doom and that all your hard work in life has been in vain, you order the Peace Corps forms and get ready to sign your name on the dotted line.

Triggering the Blues

What propels a happy, stable woman to enter the Crisis Chick phase, and why does she have such a hard time getting out of it? Obvious reasons come to mind, like a death in the family or a major breakup, but many women go through this phase without such an obvious catalyst bringing it on. You just wake up one day and feel completely unsure about what you want and where you're headed in life. To make matters worse, nothing is really wrong. Your friends say, "You have everything. How can you be depressed?"

Though there is no concrete explanation for this phase of youthful depression, there are several theories about what causes it.

Too Many Choices

Though choice is a good thing, of course, and we are fortunate to have options before us, too many choices can be daunting and push a chick into crisis mode. In the modern world, many people have opportunities to improve their lives and choose a career for fulfillment, not just money. Trying to pick the right path without knowing how things will pan out can be scary. When a girl is torn between being an artist or taking a high-paying tech job, studying theater or becoming a lawyer, she can feel very overwhelmed by the choices before her.

The Attempt to Do It All

Many women have a knack for doing a thousand things at once and they balance work, home, school, self-care, and everything else you can think of on their shoulders. Some women are phenomenal at keeping this juggling act going. They have a creative career, moneymaking pursuits, and fitness goals, and they do everything without going crazy (or at least it seems so!). But add a boyfriend, husband, kids, or elderly parents to the mix and it becomes next to impossible to keep all the balls in the air. This juggling act is a waking nightmare and can stress out any woman, pushing her into the Crisis Chick phase.

Concern should drive us into action and not into a depression. No man is free who cannot control himself.

Pythagoras

Self-Evaluation

A Crisis Chick often thinks her life is not moving along fast enough. A first wave of weddings occurs among people her age and she flips out because she's not dating anyone. An acquaintance makes the news for some major career accomplishment and she feels like a failure because she just changed jobs for the third time. She evaluates herself against other people's progress and feels that she's not measuring up.

Breaking Off from the Pack

From the time we're born until we graduate from school, most of us follow similar paths, going from elementary to middle to high school and then to college. Even after we graduate, there's a window of time during which most of us are young, single, and in a job we are just "trying out" with no real sense of permanence. It's when we actually begin making real choices, traveling at different speeds, and breaking away from the pack that life can be scary. Some friends get married and have children. Some travel the world or start their own company. Others go back to school. When there is a general sense of change in a group, it pushes many people into a Crisis phase. When so many people are making such big decisions, it's normal to analyze your life and wonder if things are going the way they should. Sometimes natural causes like hormonal changes or genuine depression can push a woman into crisis mode. If your feelings of angst are unbearable and prolonged, rule out physical causes first by seeing a physician. More often than not, however, the Crisis Chick phase is just a normal part of being young, one we must face with enthusiasm and work hard to move beyond.

The self is not something ready-made, but something in continuous formation through choice of action.

John Dewey

Rapid Recovery

So how does a Crisis Chick pull herself out of this phase and move on to a happier place? First, recognize that most women go through this time, so it is not a sign that you are insane or weird in some way if you are experiencing it. Going through a period of confusion and life evaluation is actually a common and useful part of becoming a confident person. Every smart woman occasionally questions the decisions she's making and the way her life is panning out. This introspective time puts you in touch with what you really want and ultimately makes you more confident about the direction you choose. When you feel pressure to think more seriously about your future, you develop concrete goals and a plan of action.

Despite this obvious benefit of going through a period of introspection, once you're in this mode you will undoubtedly be dying to get out of it. A time that forces you to grow is also an uncomfortable one. To keep your spirits high and your life in perspective during the Crisis Chick phase, keep in mind a few important things.

Nothing is more difficult, and therefore more precious, than to be able to decide.

Napoleon I

Don't Be Afraid to Change Your Mind

Circle back to Chapter 1 and remember what it was like to be a New Graduate facing the future and feeling pressured to make a career decision. Now think of how many times you've changed your mind since then. Though you feel older at 28 or 34, you are never too old to change your path in life. It might not be as easy to do as it was when you were 22 because you have more responsibilities, but you also have more maturity, contacts, and resolve on your side. The reality is that no choice you make is set in stone forever. If you want to change your life enough, you can find a way to do it even if you are 95.

A Crisis Chick often feels trapped in her current way of living and depressed because it is not making her happy. Once she recognizes that she has the power to make a change in her life, she immediately feels relieved and ready to tackle the world again. If you are in Crisis phase, act today and try something, anything, to spice up your life. Make a move knowing it won't

Tips for Starting Over at Any Age

- Take small steps. You don't have to overhaul your entire life in one week. Take a class in a new area or make extra time to dabble in a hobby. Just because you can't do something overnight doesn't mean it isn't worth pursuing at all.

- Don't expect your pursuit to be without obstacles. Even if you are following your lifelong dream, there will be parts of it that are grunt work you don't enjoy. Every single life choice you make will have its pros and cons. Never expect a job, relationship, or extracurricular activity to be perfect, and don't abandon it because it isn't.

- Don't say "It can't be done" until you've tried. It's easy to let fear or insecurity convince you that you can't pursue a dream because it is a waste of time. Until you've tried again and again, you really cannot say with certainty that it "can't be done."

- Read about people who have changed their lives around successfully. Plenty of famous actors, politicians, writers, and business professionals didn't enter into the field they are known for until they were over 40 or 50. So to say you're "too old" to pursue something is never true.

- Pick something and get busy. Don't spend days or weeks analyzing every possible outcome. Just pick something and act on it. You never know how it is going to pan out until you give it a try.

be perfect and it will come with challenges, but if it doesn't work out in the end, you can always try something else. Never hold on to a routine, mundane existence simply because it is safe and you are afraid to try something new. Once you start taking decisive action to move toward your goals, you will leave the Crisis Chick phase behind.

Compare Yourself to You

With so many successful, motivated people in the world, it's easy to judge yourself based on where they are in their lives and feel that you're a failure in comparison. This comparative thinking can send any woman reeling into crisis mode. Instead of comparing yourself to other people, compare yourself to where you started. Think of the things that you've accomplished, the lessons you've learned, and how far you've come. Use your own starting point in the world to judge your success today.

The grass might appear greener on the other side of the fence, but it's only because you can't see clearly from that far away.

Unknown

Ditch the 30 or 40 Complex

Take your timeline and chuck it out the window. Make sure the people who reinforce this way of thinking are walking by below when you do, so they get hit on the head. The Crisis Chick often feels pressure to stick to a certain "plan"—graduate at 22, get married at 28, have first kid at 33, and so on. These artificial timelines do nothing but put unnecessary pressure on a woman to settle for a relationship, a job, or a living situation that doesn't make her happy. People start new jobs and new families and re-invent themselves at all different ages. Ignore the "you should be here" signals and do what is right for you at every stage in the game based on your own needs. Things pan out the way they do according to a divine plan. All you can do is try your best to live well and be happy at whatever stage of life you're in.

● **banish the bad vibes** Having problems getting those negative thoughts out of your mind? Repeat a positive, self-affirming phrase every morning in front of the mirror for twenty days straight and you'll slowly retrain your mind to think happier thoughts. Just don't repeat that phrase out loud when other people are around. No need to frighten anyone.

Don't Forget: You're Never Back at Square One

Recall another lesson from the New Graduate phase that still applies: You're never back at square one. When you start a new career or a new relationship or make any other big life change, you might feel as though you're completely starting over. In fact, if you've been traveling along on one route for years, the idea of trying something new can be daunting, as if everything you've done to date is useless. Keep in mind that no matter how different your new path might be, you're not completely starting over. You bring to the table experiences and talents that no one else has, gained from everything you've done in your life. Your past is unique to you. It is invaluable and it doesn't go away simply because you're switching to a new profession.

Avoid Quick Fixes

Regardless of how down you feel, avoid taking extreme measures to make yourself feel better. More often than not, doing something extreme will cause you additional problems, not

Always remember that you are unique.
Just like everybody else.

Unknown

fix the ones that you feel you have. If you really can't pull yourself out of a funk, go talk to a licensed psychologist or psychiatrist who can help you. Don't let your agony go on forever, and do not resort to any of the following:

Drugs and Major Use of Alcohol
A cocktail now and then is a good thing, but a cocktail every hour on the hour is obviously a sign of impending doom. You can't pull yourself out of a rut if you're too tipsy to do it. Go ahead and have your martini on the weekends, but save the week for constructive action.

Don't wait for your "ship to come in," and feel angry and cheated when it doesn't. Get going with something small.

Irene C. Kassorla

Charge Card Mania
A new dress, a new pair of shoes, and a bedroom makeover might be just what the doctor ordered. But don't expect your purchases to solve all your problems. In fact, they may just cause you more trouble when you get that big, fat credit card bill in the mail and you can't pay it off. Shop in moderation and lock up your wallet if overbuying gets to be a problem.

Sleep-a-Thon
A good nap can revive you and give you the energy you need to pull yourself together, but don't sleep every day away. Your life won't change if you don't take active steps to change

it—and it's pretty hard to take action when your head is buried
in a pillow.

Food, Food, and More Food (or No Food)

While a box of cookies and a half gallon of ice cream occasionally can make everything better, a box of cookies and ice
cream every night for three months will definitely make things
worse. Let yourself indulge for a while, but if you sense you're
spiraling into a vicious cycle of eat and eat more, put a lock on
the refrigerator door and seek help from a friend or counselor.

There are many ways to help yourself feel better—exercise,
eat candy, talk to friends, see a shrink—but don't do something
you're going to regret in an attempt to fix your life. Try to take
a step back and look at your life objectively. Are things really
that bad? Realize that the Crisis Chick phase is a normal part of
being young and female, and you will pull through it if you put
your best foot forward and try.

You don't have to buy from
anyone. You don't have to work at
any particular job. You don't have to
participate in any given relationship.
You can choose.

Harry Browne

Tell Someone

Reach out to other people in your life when you're feeling
down. Tell your best friend, your sister, or your mother what
you're going through, and ask for advice and perspective. Don't
try to bear the weight of the world on your own when other

Mind Changers and Late Bloomers in History

Check out these mind changers and late bloomers. They give us all hope that we can do what we want, when we want to do it, even if it means making a career change at 65.

- Toni Morrison didn't begin writing until she was in her thirties. She is now an acclaimed novelist and the first African-American to win the Nobel Prize in literature.
- Tim Allen spent more than a year in prison before succeeding as an actor (not that anyone would suggest prison as a stepping stone to stardom!).
- Don Knotts was told by a casting director that he'd "never make it." He left Hollywood, joined the army, and didn't go back into show business until he was done with his patriotic stint.
- Ron Bass, a Hollywood screenwriter, began his career as a lawyer and went on to win an Academy Award.
- Many people figure out ten or twenty years into their marriage that they are with the wrong person. Then they move on and marry the love of their life.

people are there to help you. Sometimes the process of talking through something is therapeutic in and of itself. Once you hear your thoughts out loud, you'll see the solutions to your problems right before your eyes.

You can always pull yourself out of crisis mode by remembering that nothing you do today is something you have to be doing forever. Just get moving and try something new—anything—and soon your life path will become clearer. Realize that other people go through these same periods of crisis and evaluation. You're not alone in questioning life, its meaning, and your future, but instead of letting this uncertainty overwhelm you, let it motivate you to try new things and move ahead to a better place.

Success is important only to the extent that it puts one in a position to do more things one likes to do.

Sarah Caldwell

Looking Back

Most women go through the Crisis Chick phase and they make it through alive. They come out on the other side happy again and at peace with their decisions. They remember this phase as a time when they really thought long and hard about what they wanted out of life. They made choices, lived with the consequences, and learned that they have to accept each day as it comes. According to women who have survived their Crisis Chick phase, you'll know you're out of it when:

You Just Don't Worry as Much Anymore
It's not that you don't want to succeed or make the right decisions, but for some reason you are just a little more relaxed about where you're going and what you're doing. You've moved past the "I need to have it all figured out today" mentality and on to the "to hell with it" mentality.

Things Seem Funnier Than They Used To
You're so accustomed to dealing with life's quirks that you can laugh at them. You have come to accept certain realities:

* Summer shoes will always give you blisters on some part of your foot.
* You will always find an article of clothing on sale in a nearby store after you just purchased it at full price somewhere else.

✳ Even if your phone doesn't ring all day, it will ring with an important phone call the second you walk away to go to the bathroom.

✳ There will always be someone prettier and thinner in the world (but you can hurt her, that skinny wench).

✳ Your mother will always feel that you don't contact her enough.

✳ You will always spill coffee on your arm if you try to carry the cup more than three feet.

✳ It will get harder to stay in shape as you get older.

✳ The printer will always jam if you try to print your photos at work so you'll have to call maintenance and they'll know you're using it for personal reasons.

✳ If you brag about the good deal you got on a new appliance, it will break.

✳ Road construction will hold you up when you're in a hurry to get somewhere.

✳ You will always need the article of clothing a day after you give it away to the Salvation Army.

✳ Your ex will appear the minute you leave the house with no makeup on.

✳ There will always be a condom wrapper on the floor when your boyfriend's mom comes to visit.

✳ The movie's dirty sex scene will always come on TV right when your Dad walks into the room to tell you something.

✳ At least one person you hate will have some degree of success in the world.

✳ The guy with really bad breath will sit next to you at the meeting at least once.

✳ The one time you say "hello" back to a gawking construction worker, he'll be talking to the girl three feet behind you.

You Recognize When Other Women Are in the Crisis Chick Phase

You hear your friends or coworkers talk about being confused and you realize that they are going though the same thing you did. You offer your sage advice on how to make it through the tough times and loan them some of your self-help books to get them back on their feet again.

The problem is not that there are problems. The problem is expecting otherwise and thinking that having problems is a problem.

Theodore Rubin

You Feel a Sense of Relief

You look back at how confused you were and you think, "If I only knew then that things would pan out this way, I wouldn't have worried as much." You can't remember how you ever lived before you had your newfound strength and confidence. You are grateful for how far you've come.

You Realize You're Never Going to Have It All Figured Out

You still question sometimes whether or not you've made the right decisions. You realize you had to give up something to have what you have today. You wonder, "Did I make the right choice?" Then you look at your job or your kid or your husband and you think, "Yes, I did."

The Crisis Chick phase is a long, grueling period of introspection during which you reassess your life and your path. You wonder, "Do I really want all of these things I thought I wanted?" But when all is said and done, you leave this phase behind and you're wiser and more determined than ever to make yourself happy. You rally all your energy, tackle life's challenges head-on, and move forward to brighter, happier days.

Real-Life Tales from Crisis Chicks

66 I became obsessed with this series on the WB. It was like the main character's life became my life. Looking back on it, I don't know how I became that pathetic. 99

66 I honestly spent an entire day calling psychiatrists' offices trying to get an appointment. I must have called twenty places and they were all booked up. Finally I gave up but I wonder, what happens to the people who really need one right away? 99

66 I would tell people I had a date or a family party or anything so they wouldn't know I was staying home on Fridays and Saturdays. Meanwhile I was sitting in my pajamas surfing the Net and eating junk food. 99

66 I would talk about my problems to anyone who would listen. I would meet a guy at a bar and within minutes somehow I would end up telling him about my plan to ditch my job and move across the country. I even started posting messages on Internet boards, looking for anonymous people to give me advice and empathize with my plight. 99

66 Prostitutes used to work the block where I lived. I walked home from a party one night sobbing and when I approached my building, one of them asked me if I was okay. You know you've hit rock bottom when a prostitute is worried about you. 99

chapter 8

ms.independence
empress of the universe

ms. independence at a glance

nickname
Queen, Goddess, Chief Chick, Independent Mama

look
Cool, confident, and very busy.

fashion
A suit or other professional garb and other world-conquering yet feminine power outfits.

phrase
"I don't have time right now" or "Send me an e-mail so I don't forget."

love interest
No one, or an equally busy man.

favorite songs
"I'm Every Woman," "Vogue," and other she-power music.

events/activities
Shopping on her own, coffee for a quick energy boost, planning her future, and powwowing with friends who need her advice and guidance.

friends
People she meets at networking events and the friends she's known her whole life who have hung in there despite the fact that she's busy all the time.

life goal
Global domination and her face on currency, or an all-expenses-paid trip—for one—to Europe.

*A*s the Party Girl, she followed packs of friends from bar to bar, saying yes to just about any invitation if it meant she had a place to go on a Friday night. Then she fell into a funk, so she analyzed her life, ate chocolate, and slept a lot. But that didn't last long. Something overtook her, an infusion of energy, and she snapped out of the melancholy mood. She realized that all she can do is move forward with enthusiasm and do the best she can with her life. She declared herself Ms. Independence.

Ms. Independence establishes a plan, lays out the ten goals she has for the year, and defines the steps she's going to take to reach them. Then she simply goes for it. She ignores friends, screens calls, and homes in on what she wants out of life. She no longer has time for social drama. She wants nothing more than to focus on herself.

The Independence phase is a freeing, motivational time when a woman starts to feel confident that she can make things happen in her life on her own. Partying and living it up just don't seem as appealing as they used to. She's either a satisfied single or she's comfortable and secure enough in her relationship that she doesn't need to spend every minute with her guy anymore. So she commits to doing things her way, by herself, for herself, every day, and that's exactly what she does.

The One-Woman Show

Ms. Independence is not afraid to do her own thing. She knows what she wants at work, in relationships, and in all parts of her life, and she expects to get it. She's sassy, confident, and in control. Are you Ms. Independence? Review her profile to find out.

Ms. Independence Cherishes Her Time Alone

You never imagined there would come a time when you liked being alone. But now you cherish doing your own thing. You're taking long walks alone, shopping on your own, and spending your time immersed in your own thoughts. You love to take long drives solo because it gives you time to relax and listen to your favorite tunes. If you are Ms. Independence, you also:

* Take yourself out to eat—alone. You sit by yourself, read, or people watch, and you never once feel awkward.
* Spend a Saturday night watching your favorite movie instead of going out with friends, without feeling like you're missing out on the fun.
* Let the phone go to voice mail because you're busy doing your own thing.
* Have already tried traveling solo, or are planning a trip somewhere by yourself.
* Can't imagine having roommates and aren't sure how you ever survived with them in the past.
* Can entertain yourself for hours playing solitaire or simply drawing doodles.
* Love your boyfriend or husband dearly but really look forward to the nights when he goes out with his friends.

Ms. Independence Goes After What She Wants

You're no longer scared to ask for what you want at work or at home. You have a plan for your life and you are taking

Remember that as a teenager you are in the last stage of your life when you will be happy to hear the phone is for you.

Fran Leibowitz

active steps to achieve it. You provide your boss with a five-page document justifying your raise. When you're buying a house, you investigate the market fully and press the broker to find you exactly what you're looking for. During your Worker Bee phase you were more meek and accommodating, but these days, you don't have time to waste. You say no to doing extra things that don't add value to your life. You:

* Show up at the store for the postholiday sale and deftly maneuver your way through hordes of manic shoppers to get to the front and grab the cashmere sweater you've been eyeing for months.
* Pursue your goals undeterred by what others may say, embarking on a well-thought-out plan to become an actress, an architect, or CEO.
* Finally teach a class or start that small business you've been talking about for years.
* Make a plan to redo your living room and follow through, pulling up the old rug, reupholstering the couch, and painting the entire room a new color.
* Install the hot tub in your bathroom successfully even though the plumber told you it was impossible.

Ms. Independence Speaks Up For Herself

You start to notice that you can speak your mind (to a point) and be respected for it. Your friends want to drag you to a bar you hate but you don't even think twice about telling them you're not going. Your boyfriend disagrees with your political viewpoint but you don't assume it's a sign that the relationship is doomed. You simply agree to disagree. You no longer worry about ticking people off by speaking up. You:

* Stick to your guns and try to prove your point in a disagreement without backing down or giving up.
* Insist the cashier void the transaction when she overcharges you.
* Lead the meeting at work with confidence and poise.
* Tell your belligerent coworker that you can't have a discussion with him unless he calms down.
* Say no to tasks people ask you to do that don't add value to your life.
* Ask the people in the movie theater to quiet down when they won't stop talking.

Ms. Independence Has a Little Attitude with Men

You no longer feel as if you're at the mercy of the men you date in any way, shape, or form. The guy you went out to dinner with didn't call right away, and a week later you couldn't even remember his name. You have learned that you shouldn't have to settle for just anyone—and you don't. Now that you've come into your Ms. Independence phase, you:

* Set the pace in your relationships, not letting things get too serious too soon—you know what you're after, and you're not going to rush to find it.
* Break up with men promptly if they mistreat you in any way.
* Don't take it personally if a guy isn't interested in you. In fact, there isn't much you take personally because you feel good about who you are.

✳ Tease and flirt when you feel like it because you know you're a great catch.

✳ Hold on to your own interests and friendships even when you're in a great relationship.

Ms. Independence Is Confident about Her Own Style

You buy clothes you like even if your friends are into other trends. Keeping up with other people is not a priority anymore. You choose a house, clothing, and values that truly reflect who you are. You:

✳ Keep your hair long even though everyone else is into shorter cuts.

✳ Repaint your bedroom in flamboyant colors.

✳ Express yourself with your clothing, like wearing high-heeled boots with a funky skirt, or jeans and sneakers.

✳ Have friends that have moved beyond the "pack" mentality and all appreciate each other for their differences.

✳ Never feel embarrassed about your accent, your background, or your choices in life.

✳ Stand your ground even if people criticize you for a choice you make.

Ms. Independence Splurges on Herself

You start getting regular manicures and pedicures, buy your favorite ice cream, and even go for a massage on occasion. You've

Have confidence that if you have done a little thing well, you can do a bigger thing well too.

David Storey

come far enough to appreciate a little self-indulgence now and then—but you don't overdo it. You know when to spend and when to save. You just want to enjoy your life and do the things you want to do. In the Ms. Independence phase, nothing can hold you back from trying things just for you. Consider doing some of these:

* Sign up for the week-long surfing adventure you've been dying to go on, even though it's costly.
* Purchase your coffee and bagel at the gourmet deli because it tastes better, even though it's fifty cents more.
* Take time off from work to lie in the sun and enjoy the day—without guilt!
* Fly home instead of taking the bus.
* Buy the more expensive shoes you love even though you know you can find something sufficient elsewhere.

Ms. Independence Stops Waiting for "The Right Time"

You stop waiting for the day when you have more money or you're married or you win the lottery, and you just do the things you want to do. You decide to start living today, so you:

* Buy your own house or apartment after years of renting.
* Book a cruise to the Caribbean and go on your own if no one else wants to join you.
* Trade in your car for a newer model in a color you love.
* Take time on the weekends to enjoy yourself without feeling guilty.
* Visit friends instead of putting it off again.

Ms. Independence Makes Her Own Decisions

Other people's opinions are no longer as powerful as they were when you were a New Graduate. You do what you want, take advice from others in stride, and rely on yourself to do what's right for you. You:

✳ Move to the big city despite the fact that your parents are certain there will be a mugger on every corner.

✳ Decline the dinner invitation even though your sister thinks you're being lame.

✳ Purchase the dress that your husband says you "don't need."

✳ Invest in the more aggressive portfolio your coworker thinks is risky.

✳ Get a wild haircut without asking friends what they think of your decision.

Ms. Independence Knows How to Solve Her Own Problems

You no longer need to call Mom for advice or ask Dad for reassurance. You face obstacles on your own, resolve them, and move on with your life. You:

✳ Deal with your car when it breaks down instead of calling your brother for help. You research technicians, find one you like, and take that baby into the shop.

✳ Set up a new bank account that fits your needs better than your old one.

✳ Get the broken old vacuum cleaner up and running by reading through the manual and replacing a few parts.

✳ Confront your mother-in-law directly when you feel that she's butting into your affairs.

✳ Fire an employee, hire a lawyer, or find an accountant, all without asking your parents for advice even once.

✳ Call a friend and apologize for your harsh words, never feeling too proud to say "I'm sorry."

Ms. Independence Is Valued and Trusted

People rely on you for advice and assistance. Friends ask you what you think of their boyfriends. Coworkers ask you for restaurant suggestions. People call you when they need to talk to that one person who can solve their problems. You emanate a vibe of self-assurance, so they believe you know what you're doing and have all the answers (and you like to think that you do—most of the time!) You:

* Get calls from acquaintances asking you for job leads, resume feedback, and career advice.
* Help your parents solve their insurance problem and your sister deal with her student loan consolidation.
* Manage a staff of six and lead projects at work regularly.
* Do the driving on a long car trip, pick the venue for the party, and give the speech at your best friend's wedding.
* Get asked by a guy you work with to give his daughter college advice.

The Independence phase is a liberating time in a woman's life. She has no problem envisioning herself down the road living the life she wants to be living. For the first time, she truly feels that she is in control and can do things on her own very well, without anyone's help at all. Ms. Independence stands up straight, walks with pride, and gives off an "I'm feeling fabulous" vibe. She's absolutely sure she can tackle anything that comes her way—and she does.

Liberating Moments

Just as certain moments in life make you feel fat, lonely, or crazy, some make you realize just how great you're doing on your own. You take notice when you see someone who isn't quite as confident as you are or when you realize you're doing something with ease that would have stressed you out a few years ago. When you experience a liberating moment, you thank your lucky stars that you are as "with it" as you are today.

One Up on Mom

Sometimes Ms. Independence hears stories from her mother or grandmother and realizes just how lucky she is to have so many opportunities. As she compares herself to previous generations or to women in less progressive countries, she feels an overwhelming urge to burn her bra, or at least cheer out loud for female-kind. You might have a liberating moment like this when:

✳ You meet an old woman who is afraid to drive herself places. You wonder how the heck she gets to the pharmacy to pick up bathroom stuff, or to the mall to shop. The next time you're in your car, you are like a hot-rod driver in celebration of your fearless "pedal to the metal" self.

✳ Your mother and grandmother complain about how they never had the chance to pursue their dreams. Your grandmother insists she would have been the best lingerie designer in the business. Though that thought scares the hell out of you, you realize how lucky you are that you have an education and choices they didn't.

✳ You hear about arranged marriages still occurring in certain countries, and the thought of your father picking the man you marry makes you cringe. You toast with your friends to free choice on the dating scene.

✳ You see a film that takes place at the turn of the twentieth century. You watch the way the women curtsied in very uncomfortable-looking dresses. You feel thrilled that you can wear jeans and be very unladylike on occasion.

✳ You see a profile of the top business leaders in the United States and it features a record number of women. You read about their backgrounds and what they did to achieve their goals, and you feel inspired by their accomplishments.

How Far You've Come

Sometimes Ms. Independence has flashbacks to the time when she was younger and more naive. She remembers just how timid or insecure she was in certain circumstances and it makes her appreciate even more the spirit and confidence she has today. You might have a liberating moment like this when:

❋ You check your bank balance and your finances are net positive. You recall the time when you were relying on your parents for every penny, and you feel a sense of pride that you're making it on your own now.

❋ You see a girl at work slaving away and saying yes to everything her boss demands. You realize how much more assertive you've become at work since you started. You feel perfectly comfortable saying no when people try to pawn off projects on you.

❋ You put in a bid for the apartment you want. You recall the first time you started looking for a place to live and you were too timid to call a broker.

❋ You go on a date with a guy you don't really like that much. You say no to his follow-up dinner invitation instead of prolonging the agony, worrying that you're going to hurt him if you tell him how you feel.

❋ You read your diary from five or ten years ago and can't believe you are the one who wrote all the entries. The stark contrast between your confidence then and now amazes you.

❋ You visit a major city on your own and map out a route to follow during your stay. You laugh at how terrified you were as a college freshman when you faced a maze of buildings and streets and had to find your way around campus.

You Can Do It Too

In earlier phases, Ms. Independence was intimidated by successful, powerful, smart women, but now she feels like she's one of them. She believes that she is worthy of respect and admiration. You might have a liberating moment like this if:

✳ You read a story about the first women who worked on Wall Street, and their spirit and persistence remind you of yourself. You think, "I too could have survived in the face of all men and no women's bathrooms."

✳ You hear about a woman being elected to Congress in your district and instead of thinking "Wow. She's part of a different world now," you think "Hmm, How did she do it? Maybe I can follow suit."

✳ You hear about your best friend's promotion and you are happy for her without being the least bit jealous. You're satisfied with your own progress and sure that you will have success too.

✳ Your boss tells you that you have to give a major presentation to dozens of top executives and you don't lose any sleep over it. You feel confident that you can deliver something that will knock their socks off.

You Are the Role Model

Ms. Independence is asked to speak to new hires at her company or new students at the school where she teaches. She is featured in the local paper as a success in the community. She is the person whom younger women view as a role model. She feels proud of the person she's become and the respect she's receiving. You might have a liberating moment like this if:

✳ You meet your little sister's friend and she asks you 101 questions about your life because she thinks it's so fabulous.

✳ Your cousin calls you for your opinion on her boyfriend situation and you can actually help her.

✳ You are asked by school administrators to speak to seventh graders about your profession.

✳ Your niece thinks her life will be ideal if she can grow up to be just like you.

✳ The people you manage on the job look up to you and ask you for career advice.

Certain experiences make a woman appreciate her independence and success more than ever. They remind her that her experiences have made her stronger, wiser, and smarter. These moments give a woman the push she needs to move forward with confidence and follow her dreams. They remind her that she's in control of her destiny and that if she's made it this far in the world, she can keep on going.

Friendship with oneself is all important, because without it one cannot be friends with anyone else in the world.

Eleanor Roosevelt

Forms of Freedom

Ms. Independence feels that her time has finally arrived. She no longer needs people for money, affirmation, and encouragement as she once did. She feels capable of handling pretty much anything on her own. For Ms. Independence, a guy is nice to have around, but not essential. Friends are cool but she values her time alone. Parents are okay to see during a day trip but certainly not people she wants sleeping in her apartment for a week. She enjoys living life solo.

In its best form, this phase is a time when a woman lives her life in an assertive, take-charge manner. She focuses on what is important to her and speaks her mind when it matters most. In its worst form, however, this phase can leave a woman alone in the world. Her friends stop calling because they've determined she's happy without them, men never cross her path, and her family gets used to living life without her. People simply stop making an effort and keep their distance. Embrace your independent self, but never build walls around yourself that are so high even your strongest buddy can't knock them down. Learn the difference between a healthy level of independence and a scarier, lonelier version of self-reliance.

Independent or Scary?

Are you doing just fine as a solo goddess, or are you crossing the line by taking your "I can do it all myself" attitude too far? Review these examples to determine how you're doing:

✔ **Doing Fine:** You want to drive alone on the four-hour car trip. You set out on a Saturday morning with a jack and a cell phone onboard just in case.

✗ **Crossing the Line:** You decide to drive alone across the country. You sleep at truck stops along the way and live off the kindness of bearded strangers driving black vans with tinted windows.

✔ **Doing Fine:** You go to court on your own to contest a speeding ticket.

✗ **Crossing the Line:** You represent yourself when you're on trial for running your boyfriend over with a lawn mower.

✔ **Doing Fine:** You tell your boss you don't need her help on the project.

✗ **Crossing the Line:** You flip your boss the bird when she offers her expertise. This action stems from your new "If it feels right, do it" motto.

✔ **Doing Fine:** You spend a weekend hanging out by yourself, shopping and going to the movies.

✗ **Crossing the Line:** Friends hand out missing-person fliers with your face on them because they haven't seen you in more than a month.

✔ **Doing Fine:** You agree that your group will take on the big consulting project and you decide to get started on it by yourself before delegating pieces to your underlings.

✗ **Crossing the Line:** You do the entire project by yourself and tell employees to keep their grubby little fingers off the file.

✔ **Doing Fine:** You take time away from your significant other, going for coffee on your own or taking a trip with girlfriends.

✗ **Crossing the Line:** Your boyfriend sees your dog more often than he sees you.

Realize that you can take your need to be self-reliant a little too far. The key is to find balance between your sassy and sensitive side. Once you find this balance, you'll be able to enjoy your independence without losing your connection with the world around you.

The Ms. Independence Alter Ego

People express themselves in different ways. When a woman is feeling independent and self-assured, you might notice that she's spending more time alone, being a little more assertive, or just wearing those four-inch heels that give her a boost. Ms. Independence is usually calm and cool but sometimes her alter ego surfaces, one that is far less pleasant. If Ms. Independence gets up on the wrong side of the bed, she becomes:

The Selfish Superstar

She has been doing things on her own for so long that she forgets other people exist. "Enough about me. How's my hair?" is her favorite line in conversation. She plows over old people when she's in a hurry and pushes kids out of the way to get to the front of the line at the ice cream truck. She thinks the world revolves around her.

You'll know you're becoming a Selfish Superstar if your mom complains that you never ask her how her day went or your coworker pushes his door shut when you walk by. Sometimes it's hard not to talk about your own life, especially if you're excited about your success at work or you want to tell people about someone new you met. But always make an effort to ask people how they are doing, too, so you'll never have to worry about becoming the Selfish Superstar.

The Cocky Wench

She is a know-it-all with so much attitude it slaps you in the face when she enters the room. She cuts you off in conversation, finishes your sentences for you, and hogs the floor at the meeting. Most people avoid dealing with her at all costs because she refuses to listen. Once she takes a stand, there's no changing her mind.

You'll know you've become the Cocky Wench when people start reveling in bad things that happen to you. No one wants to see the Cocky Wench succeed because they assume she is arrogant enough and needs to be knocked down to size. They are happy when anyone or anything puts her in her place. Make an effort to take joy in other people's accomplishments and good fortune and remember that everyone has strengths she brings to the table.

The Angry Babe

The Angry Babe wastes her energy reacting to irritating people. Someone steps on the back of her shoe when she's walking down the street and she barks out "Watch it, loser." When people get in her way, she turns red with irritation. She has a problem letting things roll off her because she's under pressure to make things happen in her life. She desperately needs to take a step back, get some perspective, and laugh at the imperfect world around her.

If people cower in fear when you're nearby, you might be the Angry Babe. If you notice you're unusually disgruntled with people, make an effort to blow off your steam in constructive ways. Exercise, voice your anger to a close friend who can handle it, or take a walk and count to ten. Try to take quiet time out of the day to relax so you don't feel rushed and annoyed with the world around you.

The Lifeless Loner

She sits at home and wonders why her friends aren't calling. She feels bad when they don't invite her to a party. But then when she finally asks them why they are ignoring her, they innocently reply, "We just assumed you were busy." She was so self-focused for so long that her friends decided they were bugging her by asking her to hang out. So they stopped.

If the only e-mail you've received in months is spam and the only phone calls you get are wrong numbers, you might be a Loner. Make an effort to reconnect with the people you care about, and make new friends too. Remember that you will outgrow the role of Ms. Independence and when you do, you'll be very glad you have people in your life.

The Proud Princess

This chick moves her entire apartment alone by strapping her mattress to her back and inching down the stairs one step at a time. She's afraid to ask for help because she's certain it means she's a failure. The Proud Princess misses out on great advice and opportunities to improve her life because she operates under the mistaken belief that she should not depend on anyone else at all.

If you prefer to do the project on your own because you feel that you're falling short if you let people help you, you are the Proud Princess. Recognize that no human being can be a superstar at everything. You have your own strengths and other people have theirs. Offer your assistance freely to people who need it and accept it when it is offered to you. Asking for help is not a sign of weakness; not asking for it is.

It's wonderful to be confident, proud, and happy, but don't go so far that you assume one of these alter egos. Part of being a confident person is knowing when to throw independence to the wind and let other people in. It's realizing that you do need others in your life and that you're not a failure or a weakling if you let people help you. A healthy level of independence is not about locking yourself off from the world and putting pressure on yourself to have all the answers to life's problems. It's about knowing you can handle things on your own, but recognizing that you don't always have to. Seek balance in your life by spending some time on your own little island and also connecting with others.

There is no such thing as a self-made man. You will reach your goals only with the help of others.

George Shinn

A Bicycle Built for Two

Being independent doesn't mean you don't need other people. Still not convinced? Think of all of those great things in life that require two or more people:

- A long chat over coffee, whether in person, on the phone, or via e-mail.
- Fun party games like Twister and quarters.
- A good game of catch.
- A competitive tennis match.
- Waterskiing and inner-tubing.
- Two-for-one specials at restaurants, bars, and travel agencies.
- A deep-tissue shoulder massage.

The Magic Mix

You've heard the phrase time and again: "Men are dogs." While not all men are dogs, they certainly do share some of the same furry features and habits. They itch, scratch, drool, and wander when not tied up properly on a leash. But is there anything to the analogy that women are like cats? Whether or not they are, they can take a clue from the feline personality. Cats seem to master a perfect blend of being social and making time to be alone. Sometimes they are okay sleeping in a dark spot away from the world. Other times they meow up a storm hoping to get a hug from any nearby companion. These little furballs have achieved balance—the ultimate goal for every independent woman. An independent woman takes time for herself, but she also reaches out to others and lets them know that she cares. She has confidence and spunk, but that doesn't prevent her from showing her soft side sometimes. The commonalities between the independent woman and our feline friends are as numerous

Dogs come when they're called; cats take a message and get back to you later.

Mary Bly

as those of man and dog. Take a clue from kitty and learn the many lessons of balance she has to offer.

The Unfettered Feline

Even a housecat with nowhere to roam finds nooks and crannies to call her own. The unfettered feline takes care of herself and her needs, hiding out from the world on occasion and going it alone. She:

* Takes time every day to bask in the sun by herself or do whatever it is she enjoys.
* Has her own special places that she frequents on her own.
* Scares away critters that don't belong in her space, those people and things that steal her time and bug her.
* Marks her territory. She sets and defends her boundaries so people give her the respect she deserves.
* Grooms herself any way she pleases and celebrates her own personal style.
* Allows herself to be picky. She doesn't settle for just any food or friend that comes her way. She chooses based on what she prefers and has no qualms about avoiding things she doesn't like.
* Meows loudly when she wants something. She doesn't hesitate to speak up and go after what she wants with precision.

✳ Gets lots of sleep and food. She takes care of her own needs before she gives to others.

✳ Can go it alone if necessary. She instinctively knows how to care for herself in any situation that comes her way.

The Friendly Feline

No feline is self-reliant all the time. A kitty knows when to reach out to the world around her to share a meal and get an occasional pat on the head, at the very least. She:

✳ Seeks out a lap when she needs comfort and companionship. She never hesitates to find a loving, doting friend to give her the hugs and care she needs.

✳ Buries things that smell. She doesn't dwell on bad events, hold grudges, or allow people to prevent her from enjoying her life.

✳ Purrs when she's happy. She gives praise freely and lets other people know when she needs and appreciates them.

✳ Loves to play. She has fun with people she knows and doesn't go a day without goofing around a little.

✳ Gets to know her surroundings. She loves to explore, make new friends, and develop a relationship with the world around her.

The Independence phase is a great one to be in because it has far fewer challenges and trials than many of the others. But one lesson Ms. Independence must learn is to allow herself to enjoy the company of other people and appreciate their advice and assistance at times. Be proud when you reach that point in your life when you feel that you can do things on your own without your boyfriend or husband, your parents, or your friends. But at the same time, remember to keep kitty-cat cool by maintaining balance. It's good to be an independent, sassy superstar but still have supportive allies just a phone call away.

In the progress of personality, first comes a declaration of independence, then a recognition of interdependence.

Henry Van Dyke

Real-Life Tales from Ms. Independence

"I insisted on painting my bathroom by myself. Every time I dripped paint on something, I would paint that item too. When I finished, my father had to help me scrape the paint off everything I ruined, including the inside of the bathtub, the frame of the picture hanging on the wall, and the pipes below the sink."

"I took a three-hour car trip with my friend even though neither of us knew where we were going. We made it there just fine but on our way home, we drove over 100 miles out of our way and didn't realize we were lost until we couldn't get our favorite radio station tuned in."

"I didn't want to hire someone to help me put my air conditioner in my window so I did it myself. I ended up balancing it on my leg, had a huge bruise the size of North America, and also came pretty close to killing a few people by dropping it onto the sidewalk below."

"I was going through my 'cook dinner on my own' phase even though I barely knew how to pour cereal. I put an egg in the microwave thinking I could boil it, and the door blew off and flew across the room."

❝I spent an entire Saturday in the office trying to figure out how to make this program work on my computer. The guy who sits down the hall from me got it running in less than five minutes when I asked him for help the following Monday. ❞

❝ I used to hate to ask other people for help because I thought I was bugging them. The first time a guy at work asked me for help, I didn't mind at all because I was so excited that I knew what I was doing and had something to offer. Now I realize that other people probably feel that way too when I ask them questions. ❞

chapter 9

thewirl—half woman/halfgirl
call me ma'am and you'll die

the wirl at a glance

nickname
Sometimes "Miss," sometimes "Ma'am"

look
Appears to be anywhere from 16 to 40, depending on her outfit, how much sleep she got the night before, and the lighting.

fashion
Glittery tank tops on weekends and power suits on Mondays; anything goes depending on what's in store for the day ahead.

phrase
"This girl I know . . . I mean, this *woman* I know . . ."

love interest
A guy who is stable and mature most of the time but every now and then reverts back to college mode and drinks beer through a funnel.

favorite songs
Tunes she loved growing up, now played on the "oldies" radio station.

events/activities
Attending her friends' weddings; buying real furniture and throwing out the college futon; teaching herself to cook because she has realized that one day she will have to host Thanksgiving dinner.

friends
Her current love interest and a select group of close friends.

life goal
To achieve a magical level of balance between work and personal life.

A guy bumps into her and says "sorry Ma'am." "Ma'am?" she thinks. "Am I old enough to be a ma'am?" Then she gets carded at the bar and she feels like she's 19 again. Is she a girl or a woman? She shops at the Gap and wears her hair in a ponytail on occasion, so she must be a girl. But people at work want her to run meetings, and that's not a girlish type of responsibility. She still feels the way she did in college but she's sure she doesn't look exactly that way anymore. She is neither a woman nor a girl. She is a "Wirl."

Life as a Wirl is tough because people expect you to be responsible, and you are—but you're still having fun, too. Relatives start asking you when you're going to have kids and yet you still feel like a kid yourself. You enjoy fine dining at an Italian restaurant but you're not above digging into SpaghettiOs once in a while. Women enter the Wirl phase at different times, but when they get there, they ask the same questions and face the same issues in an attempt to deal with this strange, overwhelming "stuck in between kid and adult" feeling.

This chapter will explore the many issues that surface during the Wirl phase and the hysterical questions a woman asks during this time. It will also remind you that you do not have to choose between woman and girl. You can enjoy both parts of yourself and never entirely surrender all those kid qualities that make life so much more fun.

The Wirl Next Door

The Wirl phase is that time in a woman's life when the transition from girl to woman feels most obvious and awkward. She is caught between youth and age, freedom and responsibility, smooth skin and her very first wrinkles, which she's certain are there only because she started using a new facial cleanser. She goes back and forth between feeling like a kid and feeling like an adult, and she's not sure exactly where she fits in.

You know you're a Wirl when:

* You can sit in a room with someone in college and someone turning 40 and you relate to both pretty well.
* You go to a reunion on campus and have a blast, but then you hear the undergraduates talking about getting old—and you're at the age they're talking about!
* You wonder if the guy you're dating will ever propose to you, and then at times you're terrified he might and you'll actually have to follow through and marry him.
* You research home equity loans, tax brackets, and life insurance on the Internet. Ten minutes later you play a video game on the same computer.
* All sorts of adult problems like varicose veins and arthritis seem like much more of a reality now. People your age are actually starting to get them.
* Your parents stop giving you advice and you're relieved and upset at the same time.
* Your pet might be with you until you're in your forties. It sounds like a long way off but when you think about it, it's not.
* Your siblings, friends, and parents are showing signs of aging for the first time.
* People who were born while you were in high school are now driving, and something about that just seems wrong.

✳ There is a constant wave of marriages and reunions. Sometimes you see them as an opportunity to have a martini and live it up for the night. Other times they make you feel nostalgic and old.

✳ Professional athletes look like babies, but you can still date one without raising any eyebrows.

✳ The rental car place asks you if you'll need a car seat for your trip instead of asking you if all of your passengers are at least 21.

✳ You start to question the reasoning behind the age categories on the survey when you realize you have to check off the box next to 25–29 or 30–34.

✳ They play the music you grew up with on "Oldies at 8," but you still think **MTV** is the best network on earth.

✳ You see the toys you once played with in a vintage-goods shop but you still love to whip out a few of the new board games on weekends. .

✳ You used to wear more makeup to look older, and now you wear less to look younger.

✳ You put millions of creams, antiaging goos, and ointments on when you're in the shower but you still enjoy sneaking in and dumping a glass of cold water over the curtain rod when someone else is in there.

✳ You have civil conversations with your sister for the first time in your life but you still like to tease her by repeating everything she says.

A Wirl is caught between wanting to stay in her twenties forever and being excited about the future, her career and/or family, and all the good things about being an adult. She feels as if life is forcing her to grow up and she can't stop it. Sometimes that scares her, but at other times she doesn't mind it at all and even feels excited about it. She's too young to be old but too old to be young, so that leaves her right in the middle, in a state of Wirlhood.

The Trials of Wirlhood

Every Wirl faces a heightened sense of "I need to have everything all figured out soon." She attends a coworker's baby shower and wonders if she wants children, and what it will be like to have them—and if she will ever meet the right guy to have them with. She hears people talking about "settling down" and wonders if she should stay in the city she's in or move to a different one. She asks perplexing questions like "Am I too old to be wearing glitter? Should I be eating more ice cream for the calcium or less to cut out fat?"

All along she assumed that becoming an adult would be simple, just a natural step in her life. She would graduate from school and immediately have it all together. She would step through the gates of her university and into her own apartment and voila, be all grown up. It didn't quite happen that way, but now she's able to look back at all of the phases she's gone through and smile at the person she was.

As a naive New Graduate, she was still a kid at the lowest rung on the real-world totem pole with lots of problems and obstacles ahead of her. Her bank account faltered and she suffered through the Dollarless Diva stage. She struggled to get ahead as a Worker Bee, then became a little more self-assured and lived it up as a Party Girl. She thought she met Mr. Right and became a Chameleon. During any of these times, she might have been hanging out at the gym as the Body-Conscious Babe. Eventually, confused about her future, she fell into Crisis Chick mode. She came out on top of things ready to tackle the world as Ms. Independence. But trying to rely completely on herself all the time didn't seem like the way to go either. After all, she was still a kid with questions, issues, fears, and a need for other people in her life.

She realizes now that she is not yet a woman at all, at least not in the totally-confident-has-it-all-together way that people use the word "woman." But a girl, on the other hand, is carefree and naive. She's not that either, at least not all the time. "Yikes, what am I?" she wonders.

During this phase, you're not sure if you'll ever be "a grown up." Then you think, "Maybe I am one and I just don't realize it." You see changes in your life that indicate you're an adult. Your friends and young coworkers start families, your face looks a little bit more mature, and younger people in your office are doing things with their lives that you used to do a few years ago. But you still feel like a kid. You can't figure out what it really means to act your age.

This state of age-identity confusion happens to women at different times in life. Some go through each phase quickly, arriving at Wirlhood by 25, when they have their first baby. Others go through the phases at a different pace, arriving at Wirlhood when they turn 30 or their sister gets married or their parents sell the childhood home. Whenever it happens, this is a time in life when you really aren't sure where you stand on the young-to-old spectrum, and this feeling raises a lot of questions in your mind. Some of the questions are funny and some are serious, but they all are typical of the state of Wirlhood.

What are those questions that we all face? Is there one answer that's right for everyone? When you're in a state of Wirlhood, you'll find yourself struggling with:

The Hair Dilemma

You love your ponytail but you see other women with short haircuts and they look so sophisticated. Should you cut your hair? Will you look younger with it short? Will you look haggy with it long? Your aunt insists that women shouldn't have long hair after a "certain age." But you see celebrities that look fabulous with long hair at 45. You wonder, "Is there one particular hairstyle that is 'age-appropriate'?"

The Body Dilemma

You used to be able to polish off a large pizza without worrying—that's what the gym is for, right? But lately, it feels like your body isn't taking that kind of food as well as it used to. You ask yourself, "Am I exercising less, or is my metabolism slowing down? Can I still eat junk food? Should I give up pasta?" Your mother insists that your love of junk food is going to catch up with you. Is she on to something? Are you somehow dooming yourself by snacking on gummy worms?

The Fashion Dilemma

You love shopping for cool suits and really nice leather handbags for work. But you are certainly not above wearing a tank top, miniskirt, and the pink strappy sandals you found for $6.99. Then you start to wonder, "Am I dressing too 'old'? Is this outfit too 'young'?" Sometimes you wonder, "Am I supposed to be making a choice here? Is there a particular uniform someone my age should be wearing?"

The "Act Your Age" Dilemma

You understand that you have to be responsible. But you still feel the urge to run through sprinklers, go barefoot, and, after a few drinks, tell stories that aren't always entirely grown-up. You still have the urge to put your feet up on the chair at work and crack funny jokes at serious meetings. You wonder, "How much goofing around is too much goofing around? What does it really mean to 'act your age'?"

The Financial Dilemma

Your dad tells you that you should be putting away 10 percent each month out of your paycheck. Your mom says, "Live now. Enjoy yourself." An old guy at work keeps giving you retirement literature and claims "It creeps up faster than you can imagine." You wonder if you should leave your job and do something else that pays more, or if you should stick it out because you're comfortable. Just how prepared for the future do you really need to be at this point?

The "Settle Down" Dilemma

Some days you can see yourself with two kids, a house, and a minivan. Other days the thought freaks you out. You aren't really sure how you feel about these issues but you can't stop thinking about them. Just when is the right time to get married or have kids? How long should you wait?

These questions swirl around in your brain until you feel like you're going crazy. But when you take a step back and look at your world objectively, you see that women choose different paths in life and that there's really no one right answer to these age-old Wirl dilemmas. The right answer for you is surely different from the answer that's right for a friend, your sister, or a coworker. So you stop trying to do what other people are doing and you do things your way. You decide that young or old, silly or mature, you are what you are, and you can be confident that you really do know what's best for you.

Engagements and Weddings and Babies (Oh My!)

The Wirl is generally pretty good at doing what's best for her. She might question whether her hair makes her look too young or her style makes her look too old, but ultimately she finds the power within to push away these self-doubts and do things her way. Every now and then, however, the pressures and opinions of others make their way into her head through some tiny crevice and drive her crazy.

More often than not, the one life dilemma the Wirl needs a little extra pep talk for is the "settling down" dilemma. Getting

Annoying Questions

Sometimes questions from other people prompt a girl to stress about the dilemmas of Wirlhood. They remind her of the in-between stage that she's in. You are a Wirl when:

- Your mother asks, "Why don't you dress in bright colors like you used to? You always looked so pretty." But you're thinking, "Um, I looked pretty in that outfit at 16, but I'm 30-plus now and the last thing I need is a bright floral miniskirt drawing attention to my mega-ass."
- Your aunt asks, "How is the wedding planning going? This is going to be the biggest day of your life." You think, "The wedding always happens at the end of the movie. No one ever gets married at the beginning. Is my life over after this event? If it is the biggest day of my life, that doesn't bode well for the next sixty years."
- Your father says, "You shouldn't be taking such a long vacation. You don't have anything to show for your money after you do." You're thinking, "Dad, first of all, I have a damn good tan. Second of all, if you had your way, I'd still be reusing the sandwich bags mom packed my PB&J in twenty years ago. Let me spend my money my way."

When people in your life question your decisions or level of responsibility, they make you wonder if you need to grow up more or grow up less. But in the end, you always find the answers inside, not outside. After just a brief moment of soul-searching, it's pretty clear that you know what's best for you.

engaged, married, or having a child are events that tend to finalize the progression from youth to age. So when a Wirl is doing one of these things, or not doing one of them, it can make her nuts. She wonders if she's on track with other women her age.

If you fall into this category, take a deep breath and keep on reading. You'll soon find that you can resolve the "settling down" dilemma just as you can all the others that surface during Wirlhood.

"Settling Down" Insanity

Whether you're getting married or not getting married or already married, you face a myriad of questions and fears about this whole period of time in your life. For some, the thought of having a husband and kid is frightening, but so is the thought of not having them. Review the thoughts that go through the Wirl's mind. No matter which of these situations you may be facing, you are not alone in the world.

Will I ever meet the right guy?

You go out night after night and you don't meet anyone you like, or you meet someone but you just can't imagine yourself with him forever. You try online dating, speed dating, friend-set-me-up-dating, and in the end you're really exhausted. You wonder, "Where the heck is this Mr. Right person? Will I ever meet him?"

Is this particular guy the "right" guy for me?

You start dating a guy and you like him. He's fun, he gets along with your family, and you have a lot in common. Some days you can see yourself with him forever. Other days you are not sure if you want to wake up next to him tomorrow. But the thought of him not wanting to be with *you* scares you, too. The two of you fight sometimes. Is that a sign that it's all wrong? Maybe there's someone better? How do you *really know* he's the right one?

What if he never proposes?

You decide you really do like him and you want to marry him. If he proposes, you'll say yes. But weeks pass, then months, and he doesn't ask. What is going on? What if he never proposes?

You're the one who wasn't sure about *him*—how dare he not be sure about *you*? You think, "Where the hell's the ring, buddy? Let's get this thing moving before I change my mind."

Okay, so if he's "the one" then why am I so damn scared to get married?

He finally proposes. You're overjoyed for a few weeks. Then your mother starts talking about a marriage license. A license? That sounds so official. You have a wedding to plan, forms to fill out, opinionated parents and in-laws coming at you from every direction with bridal magazines and guest list additions . . . AND you have to sign a court document? This marriage thing is scary—you're going to spend the rest of your life with one man, this man, the one you fight with sometimes because he puts the remote on the couch and it falls in between the cushions. You're scared to death, but excited too.

Why does the thought of having a child flip me out?

Your mother, aunts, grandmother, and every other woman in your life who has a pulse keeps asking you when the first bundle of joy will appear. You think, "A boyfriend would be nice first." The concept of caring for a living, breathing little thing that doesn't have four paws scares you to death. Your thoughts oscillate back and forth between "pro-baby" and "absolutely no-waybe."

You're flying on a business trip and a tiny cherub climbs over the seat on the plane and bugs you. You think he's cute for the first thirty seconds; then you consider opening up the window and watching baby Johnny skydive. But you wonder, "Is something wrong with me for not wanting children right now? When will I be ready? Will there ever be a *right* time?"

Why does the thought of NOT having a child flip me out?

You play with your sister's toddler and people assume he's yours because you are no longer too young to have a kid. You're actually five years older than your mother was when she had you. Then the thoughts kick in: "I want a baby. Will I be able to have one?" You've spent your whole life trying not to get pregnant and now you're worried that you won't be able to. It seems kind of twisted.

The Wirl faces these many questions and issues as she navigates this strange period of time in her life. No matter what stage of the game you're in, relax and take a step back for a few minutes. Look at your life with a objective eye and you will have newfound confidence to deal with these questions of Wirlhood.

Coping with Confidence

To make it through this confusing period of time, keep these three principles in mind. They will help you stay grounded in what you want even if other people are making different choices.

Principle 1: What's right for someone else is not necessarily right for you.

Time and again, the Wirl must remind herself that someone else's life choices would not necessarily make her happy, and vice versa. A friend's life can be picture perfect *for her*, but if you were living it, you'd be pulling your hair out. Different people have different needs and desires. Don't allow yourself to settle for the wrong guy because you want to get married. Don't put off starting a life with the person you adore because your friends are still single and your parents think you're jumping in too fast. Ultimately you have to make your own decisions. As a Wirl, you soon realize that doing things your way is the only way you're going to be happy.

Principle 2: Believe that there's a plan for your life.

Call it religious or spiritual or philosophical or whatever you want to call it, but ultimately a Wirl must realize that some things in life are out of her control. There is a plan for your life, and all you can do is your best to keep moving in the direction you want to go. The rest is up to the powers that be. Have faith that things will work out the way they are supposed to, that somehow you'll learn the lessons you're meant to learn on this earth, and that if you are a good person and try your best, you will end up exactly where you are supposed to be in this world.

> *Faith is not belief.*
> *Belief is passive.*
> *Faith is active.*
>
> Edith Hamilton

Principle 3: "Pray . . . but keep rowing."

Have faith that things will work out for the best, but remember that you don't have to sit back and let things happen to you. You have the power to change your own life. If you aren't happy with your relationships, your looks, or the direction you are moving in at any age, you can take active steps to change these things. The challenges of being a Wirl might drive you a little crazy at times, but ultimately you have the power to move beyond them, make your own decisions, and improve your life.

A Wirl's responsibility to herself is to remember that she does not have to make the same choices in life that other people make. She can do things at her own pace, cutting her hair when she feels like it and wearing glitter to her thirty-fifth birthday party. She is a confident woman and doesn't have to worry about what other people think. Of course that won't stop her mother from saying "Put more blush on those cheeks. You look so pale. And why are you wearing that low-cut shirt?" But by focusing on her own needs and not on societal expectations, she places herself in charge of her own life at every age.

While one finds company in himself and his pursuits, he cannot feel old, no matter what his years may be.

Amos Bronson Alcott

The Best of Both Wirl-ds

The Wirl phase brings its fair share of challenges, but there are plenty of things to celebrate about this phase as well. At no other time in a woman's life does she have the license to be silly and do immature things while also having enough money and responsibility to do them. This phase offers the best of both worlds.

She Has Freedom

A Wirl is old enough to have some cash and a few extra vacation days but she's still young enough to pick up and fly to the Alps at the last minute, leaving very few responsibilities behind. She's proven herself at work so she doesn't feel that she needs to spend every spare minute performing at her best. She feels completely free to relax and enjoy her life.

She Has Perspective

A Wirl has the perspective she needs to laugh at the peculiarities of youth and the funny things she did. She knows a breakup isn't the end of the world. She knows her skin will not always look like it did when she was 15, and that cellulite is an evil condition that even the skinniest girls get. She no longer thinks that the problems that come with being young and female are specific to her life. She sees her friends, acquaintances, and celebrities facing the same obstacles and issues every day, and somehow it makes her feel better to know that they are suffering too.

She Has Versatility

She can get away with playing "young" or "old" in all situations. She can dress up in a tight shirt one night and a suit the next. She knows how to play "I'm just a kid" with her boss, her parents, and even her boyfriend to get out of a little responsibility here and there. She also knows how to use her maturity to her advantage to get the raise she deserves. When she wants to make her nephews comfortable, she can turn on her kid qualities and they relate to her fully. But when her uncle walks in the room, she can chat about political issues and the financial markets. She can convince the old executives at work that she has new, young, fresh ideas but that she's old enough and mature enough to carry them out successfully.

She Has Experience

A Wirl can design the house from scratch and find the builders to put it up. She can come up with an idea for a sparkling handbag and she has the know-how to start selling it. She no longer feels like she has to stand on the sidelines and learn and watch. She is a "doer" in the world, a full-fledged participant in life, and she can finally turn all the dreams and schemes of her youth into reality.

When she reaches this point, a Wirl no longer worries that her carefree days are coming to an end. She feels more carefree than she ever did because she has the money, time, and experience to solve the problems that come her way. She has the kid-like sparkle, energy, and excitement she always had, but now she has the wisdom of maturity too.

One day she starts to think, "Maybe I am all grown up and it's not as bad as I thought it was going to be." She realizes that

The Fountain of Youth

At every age, make sure you continue to do the fun, spontaneous things you did as a kid. They keep life exciting. At least once a month, do one of the following:

- Draw, color, or paint a picture. It gets the creative mind moving and can be an excellent way to kill time in a meeting if you do it discreetly.
- Blow bubbles when you're chewing gum. If someone's bugging you on the train, it can be a fun way to bug them back.
- Take a good, objective look at your wardrobe and add a little color. Never wear the same shirt and shorts as your partner and think "Twin is in."
- Dress up on Halloween. It's the only time in your life when you can wear a disguise to work and people won't think you're crazy.
- Pinch someone you love when you're angry (not too hard!). It's a good way to break through the tension and get the conversation moving.
- When someone calls you a nasty name, reply with "I know you are but what am I," and revel in their confusion.
- Tell your boyfriend he has cooties, because he probably does.

being an adult isn't about kissing goodbye all those crazy things that she did as a kid. It's really about learning to combine the best parts of youth and age and letting your crazy kid side shine when you feel moved to do so. You don't have to stop coloring with crayons or having fun just because you've reached a certain age. You can resolve to do things your way, and never really

We grow neither better or worse as we get old, but more like ourselves.

May L. Becker

choose between youth and age. You can allow both sides of yourself to coexist, and move ahead with confidence and energy.

Real-Life Tales from Wirls

❝I used to spend hours primping and worrying about getting every strand of hair in place. I was so concerned about what other people thought of me. I finally learned that it doesn't matter what other people think and all that primping wasn't really making me look that different anyway. ❞

❝I now buy presents for people throughout the year so when a birthday or holiday rolls around, I don't need to shop under pressure. It is something my mother used to do and I thought it was a sign I was getting old. But now I realize that Mom never got old; she just got smart. It's a very practical thing to do. ❞

❝The thought of "settling" has crossed my mind. But usually after two or three dates with the guy in question, I realize I can't eat with him let alone spend the rest of my life with him, and my decision to "settle" gets tossed out the window. ❞

❝I will never be too old to find humor in some of the things people do at work. I might be an adult in some ways, but part of me still laughs at how serious my coworkers can be in meetings. ❞

❝I still have more fun on the holidays playing with the gifts my niece gets than I do with the things I receive. There's something very cool about toys regardless of how old you are. ❞

❝I can't resist the urge to stick my tongue out at my boyfriend when we fight. It is just a natural response from years of fighting with my brother and it works every time. He always laughs and I always get my own way. ❞

chapter 10

thetrueyou
i made it!

The years between teen and queen are long and arduous, but exciting and fun. During this time, we play different characters and try out parts of ourselves, learning more about who we are and what we stand for with each passing year. We move around, explore new cities, jobs, boyfriends, and friends, and determine what we want out of life and what will make us happy. Along the way, we face numerous challenges and do a little soul-searching too.

For a while, as a New Graduate, Dollarless Diva, and Worker Bee, we work hard to fit into the real world. We want to do everything the right way, make our parents or employers happy, and assimilate with ease into the world around us. But inside we feel an aching need to do things our own way, find a job we love, a boyfriend we love, and live the life we're meant to live, the one that feels right. So we try new things as a Party Girl; date different people as a Chameleon; change jobs as a Crisis Chick; and strike out on our own as Ms. Independence. Eventually we learn to worry less about making other people happy and more about making ourselves happy. We slowly gain confidence in our own decisions. We start to realize that we can figure things out for ourselves and trust our own inner guidance system.

This process of self-assessment and growth never really ends, but we do feel more grounded in who we are by the time we reach thirty-something. Don't freak out if you reach 35 and you still don't feel that you're grounded at all. For some people it takes longer; for others it happens as early as 20. But for all of us, the process is the same. Through experience we come to know our strengths and weaknesses, morals and values, and all the elements that make us who we are—some glamorous, some brilliant, some clumsy and fragile. We emerge from this process more confident than ever, and ready to live the rest of our lives with enthusiasm.

We don't see things as they are, we see them as we are.

Anaïs Nin

Arriving at "Me"

You don't just wake up one day, stretch, look at the sun and say, "Oh baby, I've found the real me." Arriving at "me" is a gradual journey. The realization that you've reached this new level of self-confidence and self-awareness usually doesn't come until you again face the same situations you dealt with earlier in life. This time, you know how to handle them. Things don't shake you the way they once did. If you have a problem you deal with it, and then you think, "Oh wow. I remember when this happened to me at 22 and I thought it was the end of the world." You feel relaxed and in control now. You've been through so much in your life that you feel confident you can handle anything that comes your way.

Take a moment to think about how you dealt with certain situations in the past. When you reach a place in life at which you are happy with yourself, you deal with the same situations with more maturity and perspective.

Ó

Situation:
You find an extra $20 in the pocket of last year's winter coat.

New Graduate: You used it to take a cab because you weren't sure where you were going.

Dollarless Diva: You spent it on discounted rice at the grocery store.

Worker Bee: You purchased a leather binder for meetings.

Party Girl: You treated everyone at your table to a round of martinis.

Body-Conscious Babe: You bought a supplement guaranteed to prevent the absorption of fat.

Chameleon: You purchased a knockoff of the sporty summer slip-on shoes that your boyfriend had.

Crisis Chick: You picked up a tub of chocolate ice cream, pulled the blinds, and went at it.

Ms. Independence: You invested it wisely in your own personal stock portfolio.

Wirl: You purchased the storage box to hold your favorite movies, like *The Wizard of Oz* and *Willie Wonka and the Chocolate Factory*.

When you are the True You, you can't remember what you did with it but you're certain you must have spent it on something good. You don't think about your every move and evaluate yourself as once did. You spend money, go places, and live your life like the carefree, confident woman you're meant to be.

Situation:
Your significant other makes you angry.

New Graduate: You broke up with him because you were so excited to meet new guys.

Dollarless Diva: You used his credit card to charge a new outfit.

Worker Bee: You forgave him because you just didn't want any trouble to break your concentration.

Party Girl: You danced all night, partied off your frustration, and snagged a new guy's phone number.

Body-Conscious Babe: You went to the gym five nights a week to burn off steam.

Chameleon: You tried to be more cooperative and caring to keep the relationship going.

Crisis Chick: You didn't get out of bed for a month.

Ms. Independence: You dumped him on the spot. You just didn't have time for his crap.

Wirl: You wondered if you were mothering him too much.

When you are the True You, you have a smart, open conversation about your concerns (and then you kick him in the butt a couple of times to knock some sense into him).

✿

Situation:
Your best friend from childhood comes to visit.

New Graduate: You consulted every guidebook in the universe trying to figure out how to entertain her in your new city.

Dollarless Diva: You bought everything you needed to cook her dinner so you wouldn't have to take her out.

Worker Bee: You found a friend to show her around while you were at the office.

Party Girl: You took her dancing until dawn and then woke her up early the next day to go shopping.

Body-Conscious Babe: You took her for a jog through the scenic park nearby.

Chameleon: You invited her to the game with your boyfriend and his friends.

Crisis Chick: You told her your life story over dinner and asked her for her advice.

Ms. Independence: You made her walk around the city on her own while you did your thing.

Wirl: You reminisced about the things the two of you used to do as kids.

When you are the True You, you ask her what she wants to do and you have a great time doing it, even if it's not an activity you would have picked for yourself.

Situation:
You catch a cold and you can't stop sneezing and wheezing.

New Graduate: You called your mom because you couldn't remember what to do.

Dollarless Diva: You pulled out a 30¢ can of chicken noodle soup you bought in bulk and hoped for the best.

Worker Bee: You took cold medicine according to directions and reported to your desk at 8 the next morning.

Party Girl: You made it worse by drinking four nights in a row and staying out late. Cough syrup has alcohol in it, right?

Body-Conscious Babe: You watered down the orange juice to dilute the sugar and make it less caloric.

Chameleon: You gargled with salt water because that's what your boyfriend told you to do.

Crisis Chick: You were convinced it was the early stages of a major illness.

Ms. Independence: You kept your sickness to yourself because you didn't want any sympathy.

Wirl: You went to work like an adult but you made your boyfriend put a Mickey Mouse washcloth on your forehead when you got home that night.

When you are the True You, you take a few days off, eat soup and chocolate, and take cold medicine too. You know you always get sick when the weather changes—you have every year since you were in high school. You simply take care of the problem and move on with your life.

A woman in True You phase solves problems and overcomes obstacles with ease that might have made her crazy five or ten years ago. The phases she's been through have given her the confidence to handle pretty much anything. She knows her life will never be problem-free, but she has the wisdom and experience of her youth behind her to make things easier.

> You can't be brave if you've only had wonderful things happen to you.
>
> Mary Tyler Moore

The Practical Lessons

Life doesn't end at 35, of course, so all of the dramatic events of your twenty-something years aren't in vain. They are simply life's way of preparing us for what's to come. Think back to the drama. Remember the experiences you had and the lessons you learned from them: Never date a guy with more guns than teeth. Never stay late at work when it's seventy degrees outside. Never hide in bed for more than three months or your friends will think you're missing. Remember all of the life lessons you've learned. Once they sink in, you'll be able to apply them in the future.

The True You is confident in herself, not because she does everything perfectly or has all the answers, but because she's been through so many phases in the past and has learned from them. She has within her the memories of each experience, and they help her in the new situations she faces. The lessons are numerous, and they run the gamut from fun and crazy to meaningful and serious. They are worth recalling again at this point so that you'll be sure to take them with you as you move forward in your life.

The New Graduate

The New Graduate doesn't have experience, but she has raw enthusiasm. As she sets out to conquer the world, she learns just how powerful this quality can be. Her spirit and excitement allow her to survive in unfamiliar territory and navigate a world full of new responsibilities and exciting opportunities.

This unbridled enthusiasm can carry you through any number of situations—no matter what phase of life you're in. So when you open the boutique you dreamed about, go back to school to get your Ph.D., or pick up and move to a new city, you'll remember that you started anew once before and you can do it again with great success.

Where you are in consciousness has everything to do with what you see in experience.

Eric Butterworth

The Dollarless Diva

The Dollarless Diva struggles to make ends meet, saving every penny and thinking up new ways to make a buck. This uneasy time teaches her to manage her money wisely and it helps her appreciate the little things in life that money can't buy.

Because you've gone without your creative comforts, you'll always be able to appreciate the simple things—enjoying a walk through the park, or a great sunset, or a book you can't put down. Because you know what it's like to scrimp and save, you can also enjoy to the fullest a gourmet cup of coffee, a new dress, and a fantastic trip—without taking anything for granted. No

Well, youth is the period of assumed personalities and disguises. It is the time of the sincerely insincere.

V. S. Pritchett

matter what you go through, the part of you that's still a Dollarless Diva will feel lucky and proud of your good fortune.

The Worker Bee

The Worker Bee wants nothing more than to do a good job. She will not stop short of perfection. She works hard and pushes herself to the brink of insanity. Luckily, she only has to go crazy a few times before she realizes she can't work her life away.

Once you move past the Worker Bee phase, you realize how important it is to take vacations, put up your feet, and relax now and then. By doing these things, you show respect for yourself and your health, and in turn others respect you too. Always make it a priority to take care of yourself—take a day off from work to sleep in and encourage your employees to do the same; spend a day in the park under a tree, away from your crazy routine. Over time, you'll learn that caring for your own needs is more important than any project.

The Party Girl

The Party Girl lives it up with friends and enjoys her life every day. She learns to have fun with people from all walks of life and she cultivates social skills that stay with her forever.

No matter how many years ago you left your late nights behind, you're still having fun—planning the family reunion, organizing the birthday party, and going out with your girlfriends for cocktails. Your Party Girl spirit never goes away, nor

You grow up the day you have the first real laugh at yourself.

Ethel Barrymore

do the hilarious memories of the years you spent having a ball on the social scene.

The Body-Conscious Babe

The Body-Conscious Babe is the queen of working out. She goes to the gym religiously, cuts out junk food, and follows the guidelines of good nutrition religiously. This time in her life might last weeks or months, but eventually she realizes that she can't be a fitness fanatic forever.

Eventually, you learn to embrace the shape and size of your body and commit to a healthier, more balanced way of living. You finally understand that you're not superhuman and you don't have to be the Bionic Woman to be happy.

The Chameleon

The Chameleon adores the man she's dating so much that she becomes like him. If he bikes or hikes, she does the same. If he wears surfer gear, she wears it too. It doesn't take long for her to realize that living through him does not allow her to be her best, and it's not good for the relationship either.

Once you go back to doing those things that are important to you, you never lose yourself again. When new men enter the picture, you know how to compromise on day-to-day trivialities but stand your ground when it matters most. You spend time with a guy who appreciates you for who you are, and though you enjoy his company, you make sure that you do the things that make you happy too.

The Crisis Chick

The Crisis Chick takes time away from the world, pulling the blinds and hiding in bed for a while. Her life seems complicated and she can't figure out what will make her happy. Eventually she realizes that she's not alone in her struggle to figure out which path to take, and she's able to move on with enthusiasm.

As time goes on, you'll become more comfortable with the fact that these moments of introspection are a normal part of life, and that you won't ever have all the answers. There will always be choices you have to make and paths you didn't take, but you can trust yourself. You can't go wrong if you do your best each day with the gifts and talents you've been given.

Don't be afraid your life will end; be afraid that it will never begin.

Grace Hansen

Ms. Independence

Ms. Independence feels like she's on top of the world. She is confident, strong, and happy living her life solo. She takes long walks, travels on her own, and commits herself to pursuing her personal goals. After a while, she realizes that she can't live her life on an island, separated from friends and family. Through this phase you come to understand that your time alone is just as precious as time spent with your friends and loved ones. But you also learn that it is sometimes just as important to let them help you and be a part of your world. You eventually find balance between doing your own thing and connecting with the people in your life.

The Wirl

The Wirl feels caught between her life as a woman and her life as a girl. She's not sure if she should be wearing her hair in a ponytail or getting it cut short; sitting with her feet on the chair or with her legs crossed like a lady.

The best part of being a Wirl is realizing that you don't have to make a choice between being a woman and a girl. You are both and you can embrace your kid qualities, regardless of your age.

Each phase of your life counts as much as the last. Whether you enjoyed it or hated it, wanted it to last or couldn't wait for it to end, you learned from each phase, and the knowledge and the memories stay with you. You will always have your New Graduate spirit and your Party Girl flair inside of you. These elements make you who you are—the True You, the real you, the person you love being, the one that feels right in your heart.

The only thing that makes life possible is permanent, intolerable uncertainty; not knowing what comes next.

Ursula K. LeGuin

The Greater Whole

The saying "The whole is greater than the sum of its parts" accurately reflects the True You. Each phase offers its own practical lessons, but the process of going through all of the phases—growing, changing, playing different characters, and living through a myriad of experiences—gives you even greater wisdom and perspective that you can't get through living your life in one phase alone. It's this process of growth and transformation that leaves you in a position of power in your life. You get to know

One of the signs of passing youth is the birth of a sense of fellowship with other human beings as we take our place among them.

Virginia Woolf

every part of yourself, learn to cope with different situations and people, and acquire perspective that only comes through this journey of change.

The Lesson of Balance

You lived life on the edge as a Party Girl, saved every penny as a Dollarless Diva, charged ahead on your own as Ms. Independence, and exercised like a fitness fanatic as the Body-Conscious Babe. Each time you went to an extreme, and each time you found your way back again to a more moderate lifestyle. By the time you find the True You, you recognize that you still retain a little piece of each of these identities, but you are happiest when they balance each other out. You can't spend months on end running eight miles a day and saying "no" to dessert. You also can't stay up around the clock for five nights in a row, dancing and drinking cocktails. A more balanced lifestyle is easier to maintain, and it allows all the best parts of you to shine all the time.

The Lesson of Change

When you were in each phase of your life, you thought it would last forever. Eventually you realized that change is inevitable. Your circumstances change; the people around you change; even what you want out of life changes. What you want today is not necessarily what you will want five years from now, and it's certainly not what you wanted last year at this time. This knowledge makes you feel relieved when you think of the tough times, and nostalgic when you think of the good times that you had. But you resolve to seize the day and move ahead, making each moment count.

The Lesson of Hope and Perseverance

You faced problems and obstacles along the way in every phase, but you survived them and came out stronger and more resilient. Now you are confident that you can deal with just about anything. You thought you'd never meet a cute guy again after the big breakup, but then you did. You worried that you would never get used to your job, but eventually you were promoted. You realize by the time you reach the True You phase that worrying does not solve anything. You learn to take action and forge ahead to get through the tough times. Because you've overcome obstacles that way before, you know you'll be able to do so again.

The Lesson of Perspective

Through experiencing many different sides of yourself, you learn to laugh at your own faults and foibles. You can reminisce about the things you did that were nutty or strange—thick bangs, your leather fetish, dyeing your hair red or blond. You can remember with a smile (albeit an embarrassed one) how naive you were, and revel in how far you've come. You

● **"we" not "me"** As the True You, you'll finally feel as if your own life is sorted out enough that you can focus on others. Whether it's your job, husband, kids, or friends, you have extra time and energy to give to those people and causes you care about. You pass on to them the lessons you've learned through all of your phases, and you let the unique facets of your personality shine through.

Memorable Moments

- Graduation from college, when you were closing a major chapter in your life and there was nothing you could do to stop it.
- The first day of a "real" job, when you showed up ready to work even though you were terrified.
- Seeing your parents in a new light once you settled into your new life and trying to figure out if they changed, or if you did.
- Turning 25 and thinking that your youth was behind you.
- Turning 26 and realizing that perhaps your youth was just beginning.
- Getting the big promotion and wondering if you could really handle the responsibility, or if they would "find you out."
- Getting an invitation for your ten-year high school reunion.
- Hearing rumors of your ex-boyfriend's engagement and wondering for just a moment if you made a mistake by breaking up with him.
- Meeting your soon-to-be in-laws for the first time and comparing them to your own family.
- Renewing your driver's license and comparing your new picture to your old one.
- Living with your significant other for the first time and trying to get past the feeling that you're both just playing house.
- Attending your sibling's wedding and seeing time pass right in front of your eyes.
- Attending your cousin's high school graduation and feeling like it was just yesterday that everyone was attending yours.

Sometimes it might seem like life is whizzing by. You regret momentarily that you didn't do something you wish you'd done. But then you think of all the things you did do, all those moments in your life that you remember so clearly because they made you think about how lucky you are and how far you've come. These memories are what our youth is made of, and when we finally recognize them, laugh at them, and celebrate them, we can move on with no regrets.

know now that you won't always have all the answers and that sometimes you will need help from others. You can laugh at yourself and at life's idiosyncrasies because it is all just part of being human.

Forever True to You

Believe in yourself, and believe that you're exactly where you are supposed to be. You surely had difficult times in the past, and you surely also had wonderful times. You've had moments when you looked at other women and thought their lives were somehow easier. They've looked at you and thought the same thing. But in the end, we all face many of the same situations. We do our best to handle them, and become stronger and more confident. We learn to deal with the experiences life throws our way.

Look back on those moments in your life that are etched in your mind because they are funny, crazy, scary, or plain old weird. Recall how you lived through the difficult times and came out on the other side with greater perspective. Think of all of the experiences you had and celebrate them, whether they were a joy or a challenge.

The Phenomenal Future

Many people mistakenly assume that a certain age—be it 25, 35, or 55—marks the end of the best years of their lives. The truth is that every age is actually a new beginning. At each new milestone along the way, we learn more about who we are and where we are going. We laugh at how innocent, naive, and nutty we were at all of the different stages we went through. As we move forward and play new roles, we are better equipped with confidence and wisdom to enjoy everything a little bit more. If we are 10 women before we're 35, we'll be 100 more before the day we die. We never stop learning.

Life is a never-ending journey of personal growth, and you can look forward to the future phases that await you:

The Brilliant Boss

You have the confidence and experience to make things happen at work. You make great strides in your career and you have wisdom to pass along to younger people who work for you. People assume that you know more simply because you're older, and you do, even if you don't always feel that way. You finally run a division, launch a new product, implement creative ideas, and get that corner office you deserve. All of those years of hard work have paid off. You are no longer the Worker Bee; you're the Queen Bee.

The Wise Wife

You are happy in a relationship with the guy in your life. You enjoy his company and have a ball together. You even decide to say yes to his proposal. So you marry him—the lucky dog. The two of you plan the wedding, make the vows, take the honeymoon, and arrive back home safe and sound to start your married life together.

You know that the best and most challenging times in your relationship lie ahead. You know it isn't always going to be perfect, but you have the wisdom and patience to be a good friend to him. You teach him important things like "Trolls and other plastic figurines do not go on top of the television" and "Chips, salsa, and pizza aren't staple dinner foods." He is also a friend to you, giving you the love and support you need and deserve. You can picture yourself at 75 with him by your side.

The It's-about-More-Than-Me Mom

You know you can do it all—and you do. Whether you're mothering your kids, employees, friends (or even your husband), their needs come first—which can be both strangely and wonderfully liberating. Confident, competent, and willing to be seen in public sans makeup, you still have those core cravings for the latest pair of sexy Manolo Blahniks—but now you're too smart to pay retail.

Most of us become parents long before we have stopped being children.

Mignon McLaughlin

The Supportive Sister

You provide a shoulder to cry on when someone needs it and you can help people through the hard times. Whether it's a sibling or a best friend, you listen and offer advice to help her through her troubles. You shop together or go out for a drink and share the excitement and angst of getting older. You reminisce together and listen to each other's stories about kids and parents and all the crazy things you both endure. She is your sister in life or in spirit.

The Serious Student

You have the urge to return to the classroom, so you go back and get your Ph.D. Or you finish the degree you didn't have time to complete when you were in your twenties. You're eager to make a career switch or simply delve back into academia. You love learning and you finally have the time in your life to pursue your interests. You are an example to everyone that one can go back to school at any age.

The Free Agent

You have money and time to kill, so you embark on a plan to travel the world. Your kids are grown up or you're retired and you leave it all behind for Europe or Asia. You hit the road in an RV and drive across the country. You have a list a mile long of places you want to visit, and you have the energy to do it all.

The phases yet to come are numerous, and all of them will be as exciting and challenging as those that have passed. They will present new opportunities to learn about yourself and others. They will also give you a chance to do some of the same things you did in your youth. As you move forward, you'll face familiar challenges again, but this time you'll have the humor and perspective to deal with them gracefully.

conclusion

A woman plays several roles in her life before she figures out who she really is. She's social and assertive one minute, meek and fearful the next. She might don an evening gown and hit the town or button up her suit and hit a meeting. These phases are not random periods of time spent doing things she'll never do again, or dating people she'll forget about forever. She takes pieces of each phase with her throughout her life, each one being an integral part of the learning process that turns her into the confident, happy woman she is meant to be. Fate dishes us this multiple-personality state of being young and female on purpose, and it's our job to laugh at it and learn from it (given that it's not possible to hunt fate down and smack her silly for torturing us).

We never stop learning and changing, even once we're all grown up. We continue to play different roles—the wise wife, the doting mom, the smart aunt, the crazy coworker, the gutsy grandmother, and more. Life is a journey of growth and transformation, but that's what keeps it interesting.

So we can use our own experiences to help other women through theirs. We can be patient with our friends, sisters, coworkers, children, and grandchildren, letting them experience each phase fully, never expecting them to be where we are without going through the steps to get there. We can laugh and find comfort in knowing that no phase in life lasts forever, that change is something we can rely on. Move forward in your life and remember the lessons you learned in your youth. Laugh at the funny things you did, see your younger self with a forgiving eye, and always celebrate and embrace the 10 women you'll be before you're 35.

I wanted a perfect ending.

Now I've learned, the hard way, that some poems don't rhyme, and some stories don't have a clear beginning, middle, and end.

Life is about not knowing, having to change, taking the moment and making the best of it, without knowing what's going to happen next.

Delicious ambiguity.

Gilda Radner

About the Author

Alison James is an expert in relationship and lifestyle issues affecting young women today. She combines her unique background in public policy with personal experience to create books that entertain, empower, and inspire women. A graduate of Princeton University's Woodrow Wilson School and the London School of Economics, James has researched a variety of policy issues including how the media influences the female psyche and personal development in a number of arenas.

James began her career as advisor and mentor to young women at an early age in her hometown of Johnson City, New York. Now her work stretches internationally. Her work has been featured in *Maxim, Woman's Own, Complete Woman,* the *Ladies' Home Journal Online, The Wall Street Journal Online,* the *London Daily Mirror,* and more. She has appeared on the CBS Evening News, Cinemax, Nashville's "Talk of the Town," and in several nationally televised commercials. She has been interviewed on over 150 radio stations in North America, Europe, and Australia.

Alison James is also the Director of Finance for A&E Television Networks & The History Channel. She lives in New York City with her husband.